BLENHEIM
1704

EXPLORE HISTORY'S MAJOR CONFLICTS WITH
BATTLE STORY

978-0-7524-6861-7 £9.99   978-0-7524-6988-1 £9.99   978-0-7524-8801-1 £9.99

978-0-7524-6441-1 £9.99   978-0-7524-7936-1 £9.99   978-0-7524-6201-1 £9.99

978-0-7524-6400-8 £9.99   978-0-7524-6872-3 £9.99   978-0-7509-5566-9 £9.99

Visit our website and discover thousands of
other History Press books.
www.thehistorypress.co.uk

BLENHEIM
1704

JAMES FALKNER

First published 2014 by
Spellmount, an imprint of
© The History Press
The Mill, Brimscombe Port
Stroud, Gloucestershire, GL5 2QG
www.thehistorypress.co.uk

British Library Cataloguing in Publication Data.
A catalogue record for this book is available from the British Library.

ISBN 978 0 7524 9968 0

Typesetting and origination by The History Press
Printed in Great Britain

CONTENTS

INTRODUCTION

The Battle of Blenheim, or Höchstädt as it is often known in Europe, was fought on Wednesday 13 August 1704 beside the River Danube on the northern edge of Bavaria. In the course of a bitterly contested afternoon and evening, the allied troops led by John Churchill, 1st Duke of Marlborough, and his friend and colleague Prince Eugene of Savoy, destroyed one major French field army and routed another, driving it from the field in flight. The strategic war plans of King Louis XIV of France were in ruins as a result, and such a crushing victory over a French army in the field was the wonder of the age. French military power, which for many generations had seemed to be all-dominant, was curbed; the scene had changed dramatically and it was clear that nothing in western Europe would ever be quite the same again after Blenheim.

The allied army led by Marlborough and Eugene comprised some 52,000 troops drawn from Great Britain, Holland, Austria and Denmark, together with large numbers of soldiers from smaller German states such as Prussia, Hanover, Saxony and Hesse. Their slightly more numerous French and Bavarian opponents, 56,000-strong, were under the command of Marshals of France Tallard and Marsin, and their ally Maximilien Wittelsbach, the Elector of Bavaria. The great contest between the armies took place on a gently rolling plain nearly four miles wide, stretching from the marshy edge of the Danube across lush cornfields to the wooded hills of the Swabian Jura. Amongst the booty that fell into allied hands as a result of their success were almost 12,000 French and 2,000 Bavarian unwounded prisoners, including dozens of officers of senior rank. Such a catastrophe for France was unthinkable

King Louis XIV of France, the Sun King. His campaign to seize Vienna and drive Austria out of the war ended with the defeat at Blenheim.

John Churchill, 1st Duke of Marlborough, c. 1704.

and unprecedented, and the shock and disbelief which greeted this wholly unexpected outcome had an effect on the conduct of the war being fought for the throne of Spain that is impossible to overstate. Carefully crafted alliances were strengthened or shattered, depending upon which side of the tactical hill one stood, and Marlborough was rightly acknowledged for all time as one of the great captains in history, a true 'master of the field'.

The reputation of England (Great Britain from the Act of Union in 1707 onwards) as a military power to be reckoned with was

Maximilien-Emmanuel Wittelsbach, the Elector of Bavaria, Louis XIV's ally in 1704 and governor general of the Spanish Netherlands.

established that day, with a remarkable extension of the reach and influence of Queen Anne and her ministers and generals. The previous invincibility of French armies and the renowned Marshals of France, carefully built up over the previous eighty years, was swept away and would not be fully re-established for 100 years or so; as a result a balance of power in Europe, with no one state able to dominate all others at will was achieved. The Battle of Blenheim can, accordingly, be seen as one of the very few real turning points in history, a decisive moment; the fact that it was the culmination of a daring campaign fraught with risk and a fierce and finely balanced contest on the field of battle with all to play for, adds to the enduring fascination of the story.

TIMELINE

<table>
<tr><td rowspan="2">1700</td><td>1 November:</td><td>The death of King Carlos II of Spain</td></tr>
<tr><td>16 November:</td><td>Philippe, Duc d'Anjou, accepts the offer of the Spanish throne</td></tr>
<tr><td rowspan="2">1701</td><td>February:</td><td>French troops occupy the barrier towns in the Spanish Netherlands</td></tr>
<tr><td>7 September:</td><td>The terms of the Treaty of the Grand Alliance agreed</td></tr>
<tr><td rowspan="2">1702</td><td>15 May:</td><td>The Grand Alliance declares war on France and her allies</td></tr>
<tr><td>1 July:</td><td>Marlborough takes command of the Anglo-Dutch armies when in the field</td></tr>
<tr><td rowspan="3">1703</td><td>June:</td><td>The Elector of Bavaria allies himself to France</td></tr>
<tr><td>November:</td><td>The Duke of Savoy joins the Grand Alliance</td></tr>
<tr><td>December:</td><td>Portugal joins the Grand Alliance</td></tr>
<tr><td rowspan="3">1704</td><td>4 May:</td><td>British troops begin to concentrate and march south from Holland</td></tr>
<tr><td>19 May:</td><td>Marlborough begins the march from the Low Countries to the Danube</td></tr>
<tr><td>8 June:</td><td>Marlborough, the Margrave of Baden and Prince Eugene meet at Mundelheim</td></tr>
</table>

Timeline

1704

2 July:	The Battle of the Schellenberg. News comes of Tallard's march
6 August:	Marshal Tallard combines with Marshal Marsin and the Elector of Bavaria
11 August:	Marlborough and Eugene combine forces at Donauwörth
11 August:	Siege of Ingolstadt by Baden begins
13 August:	The Battle of Blenheim
21 August:	News of the victory reaches Queen Anne, and Louis XIV in Versailles
29 October:	The allies occupy Trier on the Moselle
28 November:	The allies capture Landau in Alsace
14 December:	Marlborough arrives back in London
20 December:	The allies take Trabach on the Moselle

Note on dating: In the early eighteenth century, the Julian calendar (Old Style or O.S.) was still in use in the British Isles, whereas on the Continent the Gregorian calendar (New Style or N.S.) was used. This 'new' system was ten days ahead of the old one up to 1700, and eleven days ahead thereafter. As the British adopted the N.S. later in the century, and almost all the narrative takes place on the Continent, N.S. dating has been used throughout this book.

HISTORICAL BACKGROUND

The War of the Spanish Succession was fought to determine who should sit on the throne in Madrid, once the semi-invalid King Carlos II had died in November 1700. That monarch had no obvious immediate successor, and in his will he named Philippe, Duc d'Anjou – the younger grandson of King Louis XIV of France – as his heir. The problem that this caused was obvious, as such an apparent extension of French influence over the wide and immensely wealthy Spanish Empire would alarm all other states in western Europe, many of whom had suffered at the hands of the Sun King and his military commanders over the preceding decades as the borders of France were extended and strengthened. An additional difficulty was that the younger son of the Emperor Leopold I in Vienna, the Archduke Charles, also had as good a claim to the throne as the young Frenchman.

The quandary for Louis XIV was that if the offer to his grandson was refused, it would then immediately be made to Archduke Charles who would almost certainly accept. In that case, the old French concern at the Habsburg encirclement (with potentially hostile armies to the south in the Iberian peninsula, to the eastwards across the Rhine where many German princes and Electors owed allegiance to the Emperor, and to the north from the populous and affluent Spanish Netherlands – today's Belgium and Luxembourg), would re-awaken. This could not be tolerated in Versailles, memories were long and it was less than fifty years or so ago that Spanish armies had come to within forty miles of the gates of Paris. In the genuine dilemma that he faced, the French king felt that he must allow his grandson to accept, while offering sufficient reassurance to his neighbours that their own interests would not be put in jeopardy. Compensation would be made to the Archduke Charles for any disappointed hopes of becoming king in Spain, with an important commitment that the thrones of France and Spain would always be kept separate, and commercial concessions in the Spanish Empire would be offered to England and Holland. With a little care, everyone should be able to be satisfied.

On 16 November 1700, Louis XIV announced that the offer of the throne of Spain was accepted by his grandson, and the Duc de St Simon remembered the dramatic and historic scene at Versailles, where the King addressed his courtiers:

> Contrary to all precedent, the King caused the double doors of his cabinet [private chambers] to be thrown open, and ordered all the crowd assembled without to enter (it was a very full Court that day); then, glancing majestically over the numerous company, 'Gentlemen,' said he indicating the Duc d'Anjou 'this is the King of Spain'.

The Spanish envoy at Versailles was then invited to kneel and kiss the hand of his new King. With some neat diplomatic footwork all might have been well, and messages were sent to The Hague, Vienna and London with assurances that their interests were not now at risk, while territorial concessions in northern Italy were offered to Austria as compensation for the Archduke. Both William III of England and the States-General in The Hague accepted the assurances given, and acknowledged the Duc d'Anjou (Philip V) as King in Madrid, although Emperor Leopold remained reluctant to do so. Certainly no one on either side of the vexed question of the succession really sought renewed war after the conflicts and expenses of the previous decade (the Nine Years War), but, surprisingly for someone usually so politically sure-footed, Louis XIV now fumbled things badly and seemed incapable of avoiding meddling in Spanish affairs. In February 1701 he sent French troops into the Southern Netherlands to take possession of a number of important towns and fortresses. He clearly regarded this as simply protecting his grandson's inheritance with reliable French troops, but those same towns (Luxembourg, Mons, Namur, Oudenarde, Ath and Nieupoort) formed the cherished Barrier for the Dutch, agreed by solemn treaty, to protect against any future French aggression. There was no fighting or bloodshed, and the Elector of Bavaria, who was also the governor-general of the Spanish Netherlands, unwisely connived at the campaign of seizure, and in doing so openly allied himself to the French king. Only at Maastricht did the governor of the fortress, Johan Wigand van Goor, staunchly refuse the French summons. The Dutch garrisons were interned by the French, and the States-General had to humiliatingly negotiate their release.

It was becoming apparent that a joint effort to curb French pretensions and ambitions had to be made and to achieve this a Grand Alliance was formed between Holland, Austria and England, the terms of which were signed on 7 September 1701. John Churchill, the Earl of Marlborough, took a prominent part in the negotiations with the Dutch, as King William's III's, representative to agree the terms of the Alliance. (In time, both Portugal and the Duchy of Savoy would also join as allies). Matters very soon got even worse when, just six days later, Louis XIV went to St Germaine and acknowledged to his dying friend, the exiled King James II of England, that his own son (known in France as the Chevalier de St George), was regarded as the rightful heir to the throne in London when Queen Anne died. Even though it was generally understood that the King had been overcome and spoken incautiously in the emotion of the moment, this was a clear and gross interference in the internal affairs of England and

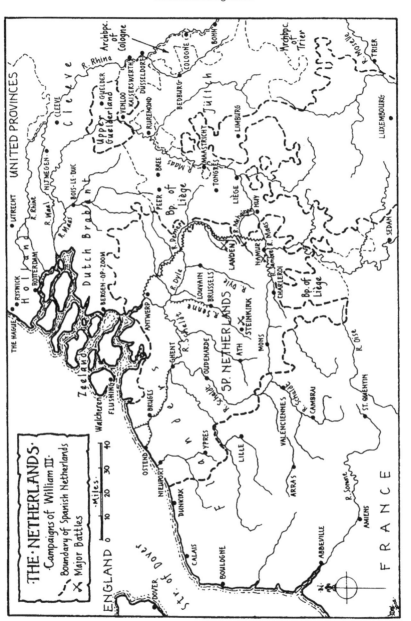

THE·NETHERLANDS·
·Campaigns of William III·
– – – Boundary of Spanish Netherlands
✗ Major Battles

Miles.
0 10 20 30 40

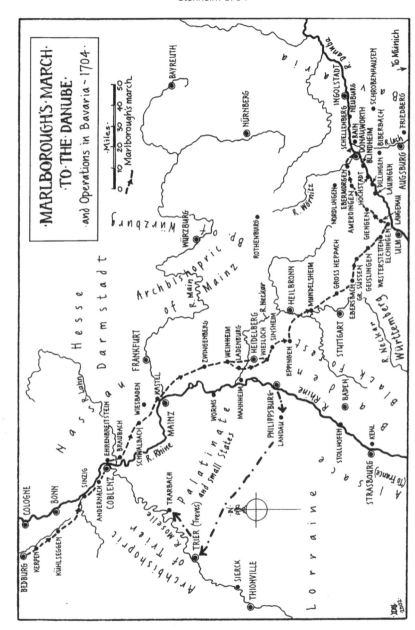

Scotland, and yet another breach of treaty obligations. The French ambassador in London, the Comte de Tallard, who had striven hard to maintain good relations between the two countries, was promptly expelled. William III did not live to fight another war however, as he died from the effects of a fall from his horse early in March 1702 and his sister-in-law, Princess Anne (James II's youngest daughter), came to the throne in London.

Fighting was already taking place in northern Italy between French and Imperial Austrian forces, when the Grand Alliance formally declared war on France and the French claimant to the Spanish throne on 15 May 1702. The Earl of Marlborough, close friend and confidante of Queen Anne, was appointed to be her captain-general and it was soon agreed that he would command the Anglo-Dutch armies when on campaign. Some other generals, in particular the Dutch, might have felt that they had more experience than the Earl and therefore a better claim to the command, but in the interest of harmony within the Alliance they accepted his appointment, on the whole, with good grace.

In the meantime, Louis XIV had not been idle and 60,000 French troops, under command of Marshal Boufflers, advanced from the Spanish Netherlands towards the southern border of Holland. If the Dutch could be quickly knocked out of the war the Grand Alliance against France would fall apart without further ado. The allies were still gathering their army together and were clearly caught off guard by this rapid move: 'By daylight the enemy's Horse began to appear on both sides of us,' Captain Robert Parker of the Royal Irish Regiment remembered. The Dutch forces and those British troops that had arrived in the Low Countries so far were pinned against the lower Rhine near to Nijmegen, when Marlborough arrived to take over the command early in July 1702. In fact, despite the appearance of early success, the French commanders had over-extended themselves with few forward magazines and supply depots, and Boufflers was also obliged to divert troops to deal with an unexpected Dutch attack in Flanders. The French campaign as a result began to drag, and on 26 July

Marlborough moved his army, which now just about matched the French in strength, to threaten Liege and the Marshal's lines of communication. Boufflers was obliged to hurriedly fall back from Cleves towards the River Meuse, but a promising chance for the Allies to maul the French army as it hurried southwards across the Heaths of Peer 'in the greatest confusion imaginable' was missed due to Dutch reluctance to attack. Marlborough, who would soon be made a duke in recognition of his successes in the Low Countries, was disappointed at such Dutch caution, but understood very well that successful alliance warfare was bound to require compromise. He wrote to a friend of his frustration: 'We ought not to have let them escape as we did, and we shall have reason, a long while, to blame ourselves for this neglect.' All the same, the pattern was set for the next eighteen months, and plans that Marlborough prepared to engage the French were frustrated by the Dutch on several occasions. He did however, manoeuvre his opponents well away from the Dutch border and the States-General minted a medal to acknowledge this in 1703, stirringly inscribed *'Victorious without Slaughter'*, which summed up very well their view on how the war was to be fought and what few risks were to be run.

Elsewhere, things were not going well for the Grand Alliance. French forces were making progress in northern Italy and on the upper Rhine, while Philip V (Anjou) had established himself in Madrid where he was generally making himself very popular. The ambitious Elector of Bavaria, Maximilien Wittelsbach, although technically owing allegiance to Emperor Leopold I in Vienna, had already allied himself to Louis XIV and now moved to threaten Vienna. The chance to drive Austria out of the Grand Alliance was naturally attractive and the main French military effort for the coming year was, in consequence, to be made in southern Germany. The Emperor already had to contend with revolt in Hungary, and simultaneous campaigns in the Tyrol and northern Italy, and if Vienna should fall to the Bavarians and French, even for a short time, then the political shock would be so severe

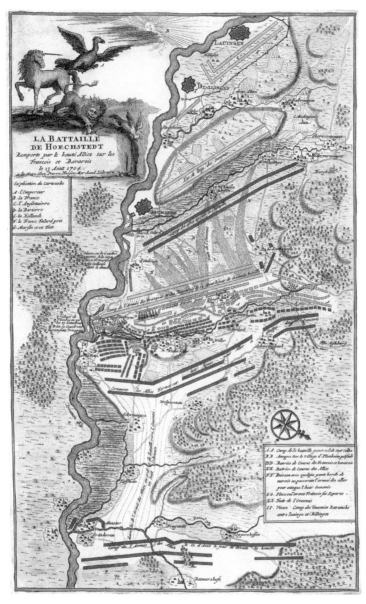

A near contemporary map of the Battle of Blenheim. (Hoechstedt)

that the alliance would fall apart just as surely as if the Dutch had been overwhelmed in 1702; Louis XIV and his grandson in Spain would in the process be triumphant. In March 1704, after a certain amount of plotting with the president of the Imperial War Council, Prince Eugene of Savoy and Count Wratislaw (the Austrian envoy in London) devised a plan with Marlborough to bring aid to Austria. In effect, the Duke would take those troops in the pay of Queen Anne away from the Low Countries and the cautious restraining hands of the Dutch, and march up the Rhine, combining with Imperial forces in southern Germany, to defeat the Elector and his French ally, Marshal Ferdinand Marsin. The Queen was persuaded and duly gave Marlborough an order to go to the assistance of Vienna 'if he saw fit'. The Dutch were understandably concerned on learning of this plan, which might take the Captain-General so far away from the borders of Holland, but Marlborough assured them that should the French move to attack, he would return quickly to their support. The Duke was, certainly, employing something of a deception on his allies in The Hague, and also more openly on his French opponents at the same time, writing to a friend on 29 April that:

My intentions are to march with all the English troops [those in the Queen's pay] to Coblenz and to declare that I intend to campaign on the Moselle, but when I get there to write to the States [-General] that I think it absolutely necessary for the saving of the Empire to march with all the troops under my command and to join with those that are in Germany in order to take measures with Prince Louis of Baden [the Austrian field commander] for the speedy reduction of the Elector of Bavaria.

Marlborough's calculation was that when he marched up the Rhine, such a pronounced shift in allied effort would demand that the French followed him, for fear of being outmatched in the Moselle or further south. They would, as a result, not be able to mount a serious threat to Holland, and the Duke made it plain that he intended to march whether he had the blessing of the Dutch or not. 'I have this afternoon declared to the deputies of the States my intention,' he wrote two days later, 'my resolution of going to the Moselle [...] If the French have joined any more troops to the Elector of Bavaria, I shall make no difficulty of marching to the Danube.' The Dutch made the best of things, and the States-General gave their consent, with some reluctance, to the Moselle project not fully knowing about a possible excursion to Bavaria far off in the south. They also agreed that a corps of their own troops already operating in conjunction with imperial forces on the upper Rhine, commanded by the highly capable Major-General Johan Wigand van Goor, should co-operate with Marlborough on his arrival there. This would suit all parties, as van Goor found it difficult to work harmoniously with the prickly Imperial field commander, the Margrave of Baden, who in turn resented that he could not give orders to the Dutch troops but, instead, had to request their co-operation. So, a major shift in the allied effort in the war was about to take place, full of possibilities and promise but fraught with risk and danger for all concerned.

THE TREATY OF THE GRAND ALLIANCE

The Treaty between England, the United Provinces of Holland and Austria, signed on 7 September 1701, had as its main provision that the Allies would seek to obtain, by negotiation or by war, that:

(i) Binding guarantees be given that the thrones of France and Spain would always remain separate (not that Philippe Duc d'Anjou, the French claimant, would necessarily have to vacate the throne in Madrid).

(ii) Emperor Leopold I would receive the Milanese region in northern Italy, Sicily, Naples, the Balearic Islands, the Spanish Netherlands and Luxemburg as compensation (for Anjou remaining in Madrid).

(iii) Holland to regain the barrier towns in the Spanish Netherlands, recently occupied by the French.

(iv) The Elector of Brandenburg to become King in Prussia in return for his support to the Grand Alliance.

(v) Financial subsidies to be paid to German Princes in return for their military support to the Grand Alliance.

(vi) England and Holland to have a free hand to trade in the West Indies.

(vii) No party of the Grand Alliance to make a separate peace without consultation with the others.

Clauses (ii) and (iii) are partly contradictory on the vexed issue of sovereignty over the Spanish (Southern) Netherlands, and this would give rise to difficulties once the region was safely in allied hands. No explicit mention is made of removing Philip V from the throne of Spain, both England and Holland having acknowledged his accession in 1701, and of course clause (ii) provided substantial compensation on this point anyway.

THE ARMIES
AT BLENHEIM

Overview

The army over which the Duke of Marlborough exercised overall command (a command he shared with Prince Eugene), was a confederate army, drawn as it was from Britain, Holland and Imperial Austria. The troops who marched up the length of the Rhine and over the hills to the Danube were almost all in the pay of Queen Anne but they were not all British, being in many cases drawn from Protestant German states (Hanover, Prussia, Hesse) and Denmark. These regiments were provided to the Grand Alliance by their princes in return for cash subsidies and were, in a sense, mercenary troops. However, they were of good quality and demonstrated their professional prowess with an ability to take heavy losses without flinching. Van Goor's Dutch troops which had been operating on the upper Rhine, including Protestant Swiss regiments in the pay of the States-General, were also put under Marlborough's command. The Austrian army was composed of large numbers of 'German' troops in the imperial service from such states as Swabia, Baden, Anhalt, Württemberg and Mecklenburg, and although their administrative arrangements and standards of training may not quite have matched those of Marlborough, their courage and resolve was not in doubt and on the whole they performed well.

Queen Anne of England. A close friend of Marlborough, she sent him with his army to the Danube in May 1704.

Prince Eugene, in theory, was of equal rank to Marlborough, but he had the wisdom to recognise that Austria, at this point in the war, depended upon her allies to a greater extent than they depended on Austria. Accordingly he deferred to the Duke as the *de facto* commander-in-chief of the allied army in the campaign. The Duke had the good sense and the good manners to ensure that he treated Eugene will all due respect, and the troops saw this and no unhealthy rivalry or resentment occurred to hamper their efforts. The Margrave of Baden was less inclined to be so cooperative, and his departure to lay siege to Ingolstadt allowed Marlborough and Eugene, who had rapidly established a close rapport, to operate more freely together.

Prince Eugene de Savoy, Imperial field commander in the 1704 campaign and president of the war council in Vienna, was a close friend and comrade-in-arms of Marlborough.

The Franco-Bavarian army presented an equally mixed picture, although they too did not lack courage and energy. The Elector of Bavaria's troops, the 'Blue army' whose name derived from the colour of their coats, were tough and well trained but few in number after the catastrophe suffered by D'Arco's corps at the Schellenberg fight in early July 1704. The subsequent campaign to devastate Bavaria forced the Elector to disperse his best regiments to protect his own estates. Marlborough had given instructions that those same estates were not to be ravaged, but the Elector presumably did not know this. Such a tactically wasteful dispersal of effort at a crucial time infuriated the French Marshals, but their protests were in vain, and the effect was that on the fateful day of Battle at Blenheim, only nine battalions of Bavarian infantry (some reports say five) were ready to fight alongside their French allies. They did, however, fight superbly well.

Marshal Marsin's troops had been campaigning on the Danube for some months and were experienced, well equipped and fit; they included a very good brigade of émigré Catholic Irish soldiers in French service. The troops brought from across the Rhine by Marshal Tallard were of more mixed quality, however. The cavalry included many elite French units, such as the Gens d'Armes, the Régiment de Orleans, and the excellent Walloon regiments of Heider, Caetano and Acosta, but the rigours of the march and an outbreak of equine sickness amongst the horses, depleted their strength. There was no remount system for the French in Bavaria, where the Elector's supply arrangements were at best a little shaky, and with the pace of the campaign quickening, there was no time for Tallard to bring his cavalry up to full strength before the onset of battle. The focal point for what would become Marlborough's attack was, in consequence, weakened. The Swiss regiments in the service of Louis XIV had declined to cross over into Germany,

The town of Donauwörth seen from the Schellenberg. Marlborough's infantry attacked across these slopes in the evening of 2 July.

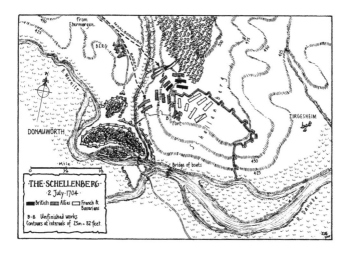

as the terms of their enlistment did not require them to do so, and the King ordered that they should not be pressed on the issue. Their place in the French order of battle was taken instead by newer regiments who, though undeniably less experienced, would prove their valour on the Plain of Höchstädt when the moment came.

This demonstrated another weakness in the French arrangements, for the constant requests on Louis XIV from courtiers at Versailles for places and posts in the army for their relatives and friends, induced the King to raise new regiments to satisfy the demand. Accordingly, established and experienced regiments were not replenished with recruits and brought back up to full strength, while new units were created. This led to a gradual wasting of veteran regiments while raw troops took their place in the line alongside them. This was, of course, not a purely French problem, as recruiting always presented challenges and the quality of those that came forward, inevitably, was variable. The allied leaders also had to deal with such demands from the well-connected and influential for places in the army but Marlborough, for the time being, seemed well enough placed to keep his regiments up to strength.

John Churchill, 1st Duke of Marlborough (1650–1722)

Born into a West Country family impoverished by the English Civil War, the young Churchill was taken into the restoration court of King Charles II as a page. He was granted a commission in the king's own company of the English Foot Guards, and saw service in Tangier, and the naval battle of Solebay against the Dutch in 1672. He then served in France with troops which had been loaned into the service of King Louis XIV, and in 1674 fought with the Royal English Regiment at the battles of Sinsheim and Entzheim under Marshal Turenne. The following year Churchill gained a commission in the Duke of York's regiment, and in 1678 took part in negotiations with Holland to form an alliance to combat French aggression. Four years later he became Baron Churchill of Aymouth. In 1685, Churchill had command of the royalist infantry at the Battle of Sedgemoor which put a grisly end to the Monmouth Rebellion, but he changed his allegiance to William III at the Glorious Revolution. Although this switch was derided at the time, he was not alone as the unwise policies of James II had fatally undermined his position on the throne. Churchill was made Earl of Marlborough and fought at the Battle of Walcourt in the southern Netherlands in 1689, and was sent later that year to retake Cork and Kinsale, both of which had been occupied by James II's Irish troops. William III was still reluctant to trust this ambitious man, but after a period of Royal disfavour, Marlborough became General of Infantry in 1701, and on Queen Anne's succession to the throne the following year he was made her captain-general, and the commander of the Anglo-Dutch armies when on campaign. Success in the Low Countries brought a Dukedom to Marlborough in 1703, and the next year saw the campaign in Bavaria that led to the astounding victory at Blenheim. After a limited success at Elixheim in 1705, Marlborough triumphed again at Ramillies in May 1706, and went on to occupy the whole of the Spanish Netherlands in a few short weeks. He defeated the Duc de Vendôme in 1708 at Oudenarde, proceeding to capture the fortress of Lille, and after an expensive success at Malplaquet in September 1709, he besieged and took a number of French fortresses including Mons, Bethune, Douai and Bouchain, but was removed from all his posts by the Queen at the end of 1711. After a period of self-imposed exile abroad, Marlborough returned to London in 1714 with King George I and was immediately re-installed as captain-general, but his declining health soon obliged him to go into semi-retirement, and he died at Windsor Lodge in June 1722.

Prince (François) Eugene de Savoy-Carignan (1663–1736)

Born in Paris the son of Eugene-Maurice, Comte de Soissons and Olympe Mancini, niece of Cardinal Mazarin. Refused a commission in the French army by King Louis XIV, Eugene absconded at the age of twenty to the Spanish Netherlands, going on to Vienna to enter the service of the Holy Roman Empire. He fought against the Ottoman Turks at the relief of the siege of Vienna, and in Hungary, where he became the Imperial commander, destroying a Turkish army at the Battle of Zenta in September 1697, in the process firmly establishing for all time his reputation as one of the great captains. Appointed to the Imperial War Council in 1703, Eugene met the Duke of Marlborough for the first time the following year, and the two became close friends and comrades-in-arms, campaigning successfully together at Blenheim (1704), Oudenarde (1708) and Malplaquet (1709). Eugene also scored a major victory at the relief of Turin in 1706, where the French Marshal Marsin was killed, but was less successful in the campaign against Toulon the next year. After the conclusion of the Treaty of Utrecht (1713) he commanded the Imperial forces still active against France along the upper Rhine, and at the Treaty of Rastadt (1714) was appointed to be the Imperial Governor in the Austrian (previously Spanish) Netherlands. Campaigning against the Ottomans once more, Eugene achieved major successes at the Battle of Peterwardin (1716), and at the capture of Belgrade in 1717. Although he retired from active campaigning, the prince became the principal adviser to the emperor, and was appointed as the Imperial commander in the War of the Polish Succession in 1734–35, despite increasing ill-health. The old warrior, a lifelong bachelor and patron of the arts, died peacefully in his sleep at his home in Vienna in 1736.

Camille d'Hostun, Comte de Tallard, Marshal of France (1652-1728)

Born into a noble family, Tallard was granted a commission at the age of fifteen, and enjoyed considerable success both as a soldier and a diplomat in the service of Louis XIV. He was cultured, conscientious, straightforward and noted for personal bravery, but his friendship with the King sustained him in high positions of command for which he was perhaps not best suited. Despite this, he served with distinction under Marshal Turenne and the Prince of Condé, and was made a lieutenant-general in 1693. He became a Marshal of France in 1702 after the victory over imperial forces at Speyerbach. Tallard had been the French ambassador to London, where his calm and moderate influence was of great value at a time of increasing tension, but had been dismissed from the Court there after Louis XIV had acknowledged James II's son as rightful heir to the English and Scottish throne. Tallard's bold operations to bring large numbers of men and supplies through the Black Forest to sustain the campaign in Bavaria were to his great credit. Still, his lack of tactical grip on the field of battle at Blenheim was a calamity, his physical short-sightedness may have been a hindrance, and the responsibility for the French defeat that day in 1704 must largely be laid at his door. Taken as an honoured prisoner to England, Tallard was comfortably lodged in Newdigate House in Nottingham, where he proved very popular with the local gentry and introduced celery as a delicacy in England for the first time. On the signing of the Treaty of Utrecht in 1713, Tallard returned to Versailles and was warmly greeted by Louis XIV who bore him no ill-will for the disaster to French arms at Blenheim nine years earlier. Appointed to the Council of Regency during the minority of Louis XV, Tallard was also president of the Académie des Sciences.

Maximilien-Emanuel Wittelsbach, Elector Bavaria (1663-1726)

Born in Munich, Max-Emanuel as he was often known, was a Kurfurst (Prince-Elector) of the Holy Roman Empire, and Duke of Luxembourg. He was a notably valiant soldier, establishing a fine reputation against the Ottomans and served at the siege of Vienna and capture of Belgrade. Known as the 'Red King' for the favourite coat he wore on campaign, Max-Emanuel became Elector in 1679, on the death of his father, Ferdinand. His son, Frederick-Joseph, had been intended to succeed Carlos II of Spain when he died, but the young man succumbed to smallpox in 1699. In 1703, Max-Emanuel allied himself to Louis XIV against the Emperor Leopold in part to ensure his role as governor of the Spanish Netherlands which, after 1702, inevitably required French approval. He was brave enough, and fought well at Blenheim, holding the village of Lutzingen against the repeated attacks of Prince Eugene, but with the defeat of the Franco-Bavarian army that day, went to the Spanish Netherlands with what forces he managed to salvage from the disaster. Bavaria was then occupied by Austrian forces and civil unrest resulted. Two years later, the Elector shared in the defeat at Ramillies, and was increasingly sidelined, with his attempt to seize Brussels in the autumn of 1708 failing ignominiously. With the end of the war, at the Treaty of Utrecht, the Elector was restored to all his confiscated properties, and devoted much of his later life to re-establishing the battered Wittelsbach family influence and fortunes in southern Germany.

Ferdinand Comte de Marsin, Marshal of France (1656-1706)

Described as a small man, very animated in conversation, Marsin was born in Mechelin in the Spanish Netherlands, and was only naturalised as a Frenchman at the age of five. His father, Jean Gapard, was a Marshal of France. Marsin entered French service as a young gentleman volunteer and served with distinction with the newly created Gens d'Armes de Flandres, fighting in the 1690s at the battles of Fleurus (where he was wounded), Neerwinden (Landen), and the siege of Charleroi. He was noted for his bravery and dash, and in 1693 became a major-general. The following year he was made a member of the Order of St Louis in the same ceremony in which Sébastien le Prestre de Vauban received the award. In 1701 Marsin was appointed the French Ambassador to Phillip V of Spain (Duc d'Anjou), and fought at the Battle of Luzzara, the capture of Landau and Breisach, and shared in the victory of Speyerbach in 1703, after which he was made a Marshal of France. As French commander in Bavaria in early 1704, he worked well with the Elector, but the divided command that resulted from Marshal Tallard's arrival was unsatisfactory and contributed to the defeat at Blenheim. His stout defence of the centre of the Franco-Bavarian position, saved his own troops and those of the Elector of Bavaria from the utter defeat suffered by Tallard. After serving very capably in Alsace during 1705, Marsin was sent the next year to northern Italy, with the Duc d'Orleans nominally in command, to combat Prince Eugene and Victor-Amadeus, Duke of Savoy. He fought well at the siege of Turin that September, where he was defeated and mortally wounded.

Louis-Guillaume, Margrave of Baden
(1655-1707)

Godson of King Louis XIV, he was known as 'Turken Louis' for his valiant exploits in the campaigns against the Ottomans during the siege of Vienna. The Imperial field commander at the Schellenberg in July 1704, he astutely led his Imperial grenadiers on the crucial flank attack which decided the day, and he was wounded by a musket ball in the foot. He was not present at the Battle of Blenheim but engaged instead in the siege of Ingolstadt. Baden then conducted a lacklustre siege of Landau in Alsace throughout the autumn of 1704. The wound to his foot never really healed, a malady becoming known rather derisively as 'Margrave's Toe'. He failed to support Marlborough's Moselle campaign in 1705, and had to retire from active campaigning, dying two years later.

THE WINGS OF AN ARMY

In the early eighteenth century, it was common practice for armies on campaign to comprise two 'wings', which functioned in a similar way to modern army corps, except that they were not self-sufficient and would not usually operate independently. Each wing would be under the command of a general officer of broadly equivalent rank, each of whom would report to the army commander. In the summer of 1704, the allied army at Blenheim comprised Prince Eugene's wing on the right of the line, and Marlborough's wing on the left. Eugene deferred to Marlborough as the *de-facto* commander-in-chief in the planning and execution of the battle, an arrangement that worked very well due to the harmonious relationship at which the two men had quickly arrived. Eugene threw his smaller wing into expensive attacks to fix his opponents around Lutzingen and prevent co-operation between the different parts, operating as 'wings' of the Franco-Bavarian army. Marlborough was, in consequence, able to concentrate on Tallard's cavalry with little concern, apart from one decidedly shaky moment, for the security of his own right flank. Marshal Tallard, Marshal Marsin and the Elector of Bavaria, however, operated very differently.

The Elector, by virtue of his rank, was the more senior commander, but had the fewest troops on the field of battle, having wastefully dispersed them to protect his own estates from allied raiders. The two French commanders paid lip-service to deferring to him, but in fact operated as they each saw fit, with little real co-operation between the three parts of their combined army. To a certain degree this was due to concern at the equine infection in the ranks of Tallard's cavalry and, although Marsin had detached some squadrons to reinforce Tallard at the onset of the battle, he felt unable to move further to support the right wing late in the afternoon. Unlike their allied opponents, the French and Bavarian commanders fought their own separate battles, as if the success of the others had no meaning or importance to them, and they suffered the consequences. In a wider sense, care should be taken when reading accounts of armies at the time, as a 'right wing' or 'left wing' were simple titles without meaning as to the actual manoeuvres taking place. So, the right wing of an army might be holding a position on the left while the left wing put in an attack on the right!

The allied Army – Anglo–Dutch and Imperial Austrian (See Orders of Battle pp 137–153)

52,000 men and 60 guns (excluding mortars).

The French and Bavarian Army

56,000 men and 90 guns (excluding mortars).

Battle Tactics and Drills

The Horse

At the beginning of the eighteenth century, the cavalry (the Horse) was still regarded as the battle-winning arm, although its power to dominate a field and dictate events, so evident under commanders such as Marshal Turenne and Marshal Luxembourg, was diminishing in the face of improved infantry weaponry and tactics. The speed and striking power of mounted troops had long proved effective, with the employment of mobility and shock action to overwhelm opponents fighting on foot. The principal weapon of the cavalry was the sword, as the use of the lance had not yet been revived in western Europe. The use of cold steel had evolved over the previous thirty years or so before Blenheim, being more effective than the rather feeble firearms the horse-pistol and the carbine, able to be carried by horsemen. Shock action, delivered at the right moment and in a highly disciplined way, was the key to success, driving an opponent into hopeless flight before your own massed squadrons that (crucially) maintained their order and conserved their strength for further efforts. The French cavalry, in particular, clung longer than most others to the outdated use of firearms discharged at the halt, and this disrupted their forward progress and enfeebled any attempt to deliver the necessary shock action. The Duke of Marlborough would not permit his cavalry to operate in this way, and it was reported that his troopers would only be issued with three rounds of ammunition for their pistols, for use when on sentry and picquet duty or out foraging.

Cavalry in all armies were organised into troops each about 60 to 65 men strong, and six of these would comprise a regiment of Horse (with certain variations depending upon where they were recruited, and French troops were rather smaller). These troops were grouped for tactical purposes into squadrons, according to circumstances, but squadrons would often be used on detached duties and grouped with other squadrons as necessary to achieve a certain task. So, for all the troops in any given regiment to operate together at any one time would be quite unusual.

Cavalry regiments were costly to maintain, and troopers were paid more than their comrades who fought on foot. Good horsemen were not easy to find, and hard to replace, so their tactical employment where heavy losses were likely called for careful thought before they were committed. Given the expense of maintaining regiments of Horse, the use of dragoons was increasing. These soldiers were effectively mounted infantry, with a highly useful dual tactical role. They were mustered into troops in the same way as the cavalry, but their horses were

FIRING FROM THE HALT

The outmoded practice of cavalry stopping to fire their horse-pistols and carbines, which had been prevalent the seventeenth century, had been replaced by 1704 by the charge 'sword in hand' to make the most of the speed and shock effect of a cavalry charge. The Duke of Marlborough was so concerned that his horsemen should not stop to fire that only three rounds of pistol ammunition were issued at the start of a campaign, for use when patrolling or on picquet duty. The French, however, still used the stopping to fire technique and this hampered their efforts to overcome the rush of allied cavalry.

rather smaller and therefore cheaper to obtain, and the rates of pay for dragoons was lower than for true cavalry, so there were additional inducements to have more of them. The dragoons were equipped very much as the infantry, although they usually wore boots rather than shoes and they were employed in scouting, outpost work; when dismounted as infantry, they fought with musket and bayonet. They could also operate when mounted alongside their true cavalry comrades, who could not fight on foot, and so in both roles the mobility of dragoons was a valuable asset. However, the necessity to have horse handlers when dismounted reduced their fighting strength by as much as a quarter. Despite their dual role, the trend for dragoons to be regarded as cavalry, and to operate as such, was growing.

The Foot

Usually considered to be a more humble type of soldier than the cavalry, the infantry (the Foot) soldiers of any army were, in 1704 as now, the only combat arm capable of taking and holding ground for any length of time. They were, as a result, the rock on which any commander stood and infantry tactics had developed significantly during the latter half of the seventeenth century. The introduction of the reliable flintlock musket and socket bayonet attachment had finally brought about the demise of the pikeman on the battlefield, and foot soldiers, hitherto vulnerable to cavalry attack, could now stand their ground with a fair chance of success as long as their order and discipline held. The flintlock musket also raised the likely rate of fire of musketry significantly, with three rounds a minute expected as long as the flint lasted and the barrel did not become too foul with unburnt powder. Effectively delivered firepower became a reality, with disciplined volleys of musketry scouring the battlefield; a technique even evolved with soldiers in rear ranks loading muskets and passing them forward for those in the front rank to use, so as to maintain a hot rate of fire.

Rapidity of fire was admirable, but accuracy and effect was something different. The muskets in common use were, contrary to popular belief, quite accurate out to about 300 metres if used with care, a well rammed charge and a good flint. However, soldiers were not taught to aim at a particular opponent, but each to discharge their weapon *en masse*, on command and in a general direction – the effect was to be achieved by the volume of fire rather than the individual effort. The smoke obscuration on any battlefield from the use of black powder was considerable and the temptation to load, present and fire at the best rate, so doing the most damage to an opponent with the very same purpose, was strong. Much musketry could, accordingly, sometimes produce only modest results.

At first the foot soldiers who would be drawn up in five ranks in the French army, just three ranks in the British and Dutch armies, would fire by rank all at the same time: front rank, second rank, third rank, and so on. Such a procedure was difficult to control, particularly in the heat, noise and excitement of a battlefield, and so by 1700 a new system was devised and taught which was known as 'platoon firing'. This involved the 13 platoons in a battalion (each platoon about thirty–thirty-five men strong) firing together in a well-ordered group sequence on word of command or roll of the drums. As a general rule, the kneeling front rank would reserve their fire until the decisive moment or to counter a sudden threat such as a rush of enemy cavalry. The weight of each volley in this platoon firing system was naturally less than with whole ranks, but the effect was better as non-commissioned officers (NCOs) could better ensure that soldiers were not firing high, and the opposing troops were never free from the tormenting lash of musketry delivered. So effective was the platoon firing when compared to that of volley firing, that the Bavarian army introduced the same system shortly after the Battle at Blenheim, while the French – after some reluctance – did so unofficially in 1708. It would, however, be another forty years before they did so formally.

The Gunners

The tactical use of artillery at the start of the eighteenth century was that of a cumbersome and static arm, with guns that had heavy carriages and crews who were often comprised of civilian contractors, under the supervision of a few specialist officers and NCOs. These men were well paid for their undoubtedly useful services, but their *esprit de corps* may have been a little sketchy and the Comte de Merode-Westerloo wrote of having to prevent some French gunners from leaving the field at Blenheim as Marlborough's cavalry advanced: 'I noticed them trying to sneak off'. Still, it is only fair to say that the gun crews often displayed notable bravery under fire. The trend to have professional gun crews was growing, certainly in France, and would soon become more widespread.

'*The British Infantry Advance on Blindheim Village*', *13 August 1704, by Richard Simkin.*

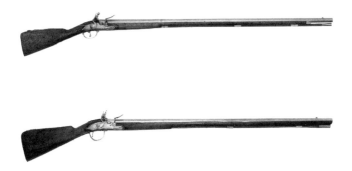

Flintlock muskets. With a good flint a trained soldier was expected to achieve a rate of fire of three shots a minute. Wooden ram rods were in use, which tended to break and were eventually replaced by iron ram rods.

The field artillery, guns usually firing six-, nine- and twelve-pound round-shot, were grouped into batteries each of six or eight pieces. The method of employment was to drag these pieces into place at some convenient spot where a decent field of fire could be had, and fight them from there, no matter what happened during the action. The sheer weight of the guns did not make for easy movement, nor were the tactics developed to facilitate such mobility, although this was largely down to the individual commanders on the spot. Marlborough had Colonel Blood manhandle several field guns across the Nebel stream during the fighting at Blenheim, and moved another battery into position to counter a forward movement by Marshal Marsin's cavalry near to Oberglau, but this was unusual.

Field guns fired cast-iron round-shot at ranges over 200 metres, as long as observation of the effect could be had – ammunition was expensive and was not to be just fired away blindly in hopes of hitting something. This difficulty was experienced by the French gunners at Blenheim, who had to contend both with the slope leading down from the Plain of Höchstädt, and also with the obscuring effect of the long and still un-harvested crops. One French battery commander got around the difficulty by firing obliquely across the slope from the outskirts of Blindheim village. At closer ranges, tin cans filled with musket balls – a type of munition known as canister – could be used and these acted like giant shot-guns, spraying their projectiles with deadly effect particularly against massed troops whether Horse or Foot. The breaching power of canister when used on light field defences at close range, was also very effective.

Louis-Guillaume, Margrave of Baden. A veteran of wars of against the Ottomans, he was known as 'Turken Louis'. Baden commanded the Imperial troops at the Schellenberg, where he was wounded.

Battles in the open were uncommon at the time, and most campaigns involved one or more siege operations. These operations required heavy battering artillery – eighteen, twenty-four and thirty-two pounders – to reduce the defences, and Marlborough's attack on the minor fortress of Rain soon after the battle at the Schellenberg in July 1704, was hampered by a lack of these large pieces. He had been assured by the Margrave of Baden that a siege 'train' would be available but this was not so, and to the Duke's frustration there was a delay while twenty-four-pounder battering guns were brought forward from Nuremberg. Howitzers and mortars firing at high angle were also required for siege work, and these used explosive shell (hollowed out round-shot filled with gunpowder or musket balls and fitted with a fuze). The ability of these weapons to search into dead ground and engage enemy troops sheltering behind defences was valuable, but they had very little real employment in battle in open field.

To prepare and supply artillery on campaign, with all the necessary wagons, ammunition, slow match, draught animals and fodder was an enormous undertaking and the slowness of moving a 'train' of artillery, dragging the heavy guns along the bad roads of the time, could delay the movement of a whole army, and even dictate the pace of a campaign. The Duke of Marlborough brought his field pieces all the way from the Low Countries, a significant feat of logistics and organisation, but Marshal Tallard did the same with his march through the Black Forest, so the practical moving of artillery on campaign was clearly, at many levels, a well-practised and highly skilled art.

The use of more mobile field guns (what would become known in time as horse artillery) had not yet been developed, although the gun carriages were becoming progressively lighter as time went on. It should be added that pairs of small 'battalion' guns – light pieces of one and two pounder capability – accompanied the infantry and could on occasion be quite effective with canister shot at very close range. These gun crews, drawn from the ranks of the battalion itself, would be operating very close to the firing line and were exposed to their opponent's musketry.

The Engineers

There was no formal corps of engineers at this time, although these were gradually developing in all armies, and most engineer officers were 'double–hatted' in that they held regimental appointments as well as that of their more specialised duties. They and their NCOs would supervise squads of soldiers, contractors and those impressed civilians who had not been nimble enough to make themselves scarce, in carrying out engineering and pioneer tasks. By 1704 most armies had formed squads of specialist pioneers to work on roads and preparing entrenchments, but these were considered as lowly tasks and often formed a punishment for miscreant soldiers. At a tactical level, mobility and counter-mobility – the essential requirement of any army on the move – was of particular importance in the Danube campaign. Roads were usually poor, and the engineers had the task to prepare a route to be taken and remove obstacles. The achievement of Tallard's engineer officers in bringing his army twice through the narrow passes of the Black Forest was notable, while the many wide rivers in the region provided both protection for an army on the defensive and a significant hurdle to be crossed when on the advance. The importance of the crossing over the Danube at Donauwörth brought about the bitterly fought Schellenberg battle, while smaller rivers such the Worntiz also required bridging – a fit man might wade across, but an army with all its gear required bridges to do so in good order.

The engineer pontoon train, the 'tin boats' as they are often referred to in accounts of this campaign, was an invaluable asset for an army commander. Although cumbersome to move, the pontoons on which the plank bridges rested could be laid across wide rivers quite quickly, and give an army mobility, while stripping away the protection looked for by an opponent who was seeking shelter behind the water barrier. The loss of the Bavarian pontoon train, abandoned on the banks of the Danube in the aftermath of the defeat at the Schellenberg, was a severe loss to the Elector and his army, and his withdrawal with Marshal Marsin behind the shelter of the River Lech gave only a temporary respite with the allies moving swiftly across the Danube and thrusting deep into Bavaria itself. 'We are now got into Bavaria, over two great rivers [Worntiz and Danube], without any opposition so that the Elector must soon come to terms, or run the risk of having his whole country ruined.' The Duke of Marlborough would undoubtedly have made good use of the valuable captured material in his campaign, crossing the Lech to engage the Elector, had Marshal Tallard not arrived from Alsace in early August to forestall him.

The Staff

Considering the numerous complex duties that an army commander had to perform, both routine and the unexpected – planning a campaign and a march timetable, gathering stores and munitions, gaining intelligence of enemy movements and intentions, consulting with allies and on the day of battle issuing orders, controlling movement under fire, encouraging flagging officers and soldiers alike – and many of other demanding and simultaneous tasks, the very small size of the staff available and employed by generals in all armies in 1704 is surprising. An enormous burden was placed on the commanding general as a result. All senior officers would have aides-de-camp in their retinue, hard-riding well-bred young men who hoped to make a name for themselves in the practice of war, and in addition certain specialist officers as close confidantes. Marshal Tallard had the services of the Marquis de la Frequeliére as his aggressive and highly competent artillery commander, while Marlborough employed William Cadogan as his quartermaster-general and *de facto* chief of staff. The Duke lost Johan Wigand van Goor at the Schellenberg, and wrote of his regret that he no longer had the use of that valuable officer's efficient staff work. Life on the staff was certainly no safe sinecure as these officers were conspicuously mounted and often to be found in the most exposed spot while carrying out their duties. William, Lord North and Grey, an aide-de-camp to Marlborough, lost his right hand in the fighting for Blindheim village, while Marshal Tallard's own son was pistolled at his side in the closing phase of the great battle.

William, 1st Earl Cadogan, was Marlborough's capable quartermaster-general and chief of staff. Having served through all the Duke's campaigns, Cadogan succeeded Marlborough as Master-General of the Ordnance.

Major-General William, Lord North and Grey. His regiment fought at Blenheim but he served on Marlborough's staff during the battle. He was seriously wounded in the battle and lost a hand.

AIDES-DE-CAMP AND RUNNING FOOTMEN

The ability of an army commander in the eighteenth century to control a battle depended on the gathering and passage of information, and the issuing of relevant orders, in what were usually very confusing circumstances. All general officers had aides-de-camp, well-mounted young noblemen looking to make a reputation and career for themselves in the service of some great man. These aides would ride about the field of battle, carrying orders and instructions to subordinate commanders, and bring back up-to-date information to their general. The Duke of Marlborough also had the use of a small corps of running footmen, clad in his own livery, who would move swiftly about the battlefield on foot, less conspicuous and therefore less vulnerable than the mounted aides, and carrying out a very similar range of duties. The effectiveness of these footmen, however, may be questioned, as it does not seem that other commanders found it worthwhile to follow Marlborough's example.

Logistics

To pay, feed, clothe, administer and organise an army on campaign for months on end was a complex and demanding business, before even allowing for the unwelcome attentions of an opponent. The armies engaged in the 1704 campaign managed their logistical arrangements rather differently from each other. Marlborough's preparations for the march from the Low Countries were admirably complete and, once he had passed over the mountains of the Swabian Jura, he was able to have new lines of supply and communication into central Germany, well away from the risk of French interference. He was able to pay for what was required in hard cash and supplies for his army were, as a result, readily available although the price did go up as the campaign progressed and merchants and farmers saw their opportunity to make the most of things. The Duke's Imperial allies were not so well placed

Marlborough's attack on the Schellenberg. (From the tapestry in Blenheim Palace. By kind permission of His Grace the Duke of Marlborough)

and were short of money and depended on their allies for much of what was required to press onward. This imposed a strain on Marlborough's logistical arrangements and he was well aware that both England and Holland had paid substantial financial subsidies to the Emperor, but these had apparently been spent in putting down a rebellion in Hungary rather than countering the threat from Bavaria.

The Elector was of course operating in his own territory, but this was both a blessing and a handicap. He could levy supplies from his farmers, tenants and peasants and did so with some ruthlessness, but the ability of the region to support his troops and two French armies (those of Marsin and Tallard), was a strain. The French method of gathering supplies and feeding their troops on campaign was robust – they took what was needed when and where they could. In part at least this was a necessity for the French treasury had no ability to dispense large sums of money to campaigning generals. Also, this method of operating was not seen as all that ruthless by the standards of the day;

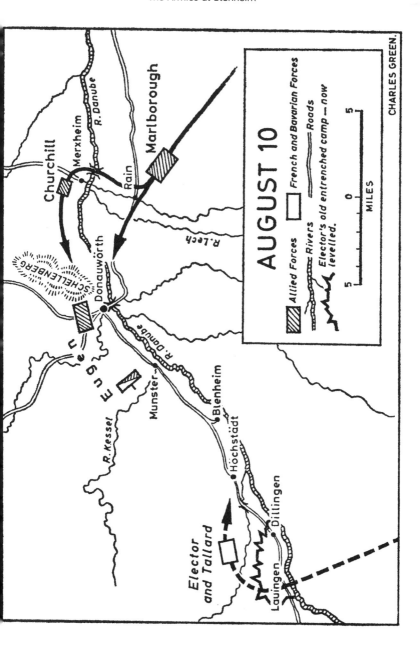

CHARLES GREEN.

AUGUST 10

French and Bavarian Forces

Roads

Allied Forces

Rivers

Elector's old entrenched camp — now levelled.

MILES

5   0   5

Marlborough

R. Danube

Merxheim

Churchill

Rain

R. Lech

SCHELLENBERG

Donauwörth

Eugene

R. Danube

Munster-

R. Kessel

Blenheim

Höchstädt

Dillingen

Elector
and Tallard

Lauingen

war was a tough business. Still, the inevitable disadvantage was that locals would hide their supplies or actively resist as far as they were able, while they would welcome Marlborough's quartermasters. In either case, logistics remained as essential part of any campaign – an army that was not fed was soon a mob, not an army at all.

The Medical Services

Medical care for sick and wounded was available, but it was of a fairly rudimentary nature in 1704, so it is as well that the soldiers were generally of tough stock. Prior to the assault on the Schellenberg, Marlborough made arrangements for the reception of wounded at his forward base which was then at Nördlingen 'He then sent an express to the commissary of the hospital to hasten them to Nördlingen, and to march day and night, 'till he had settled with it there. This express was followed by two more, to hasten the apothecaries and surgeons.' Once the armies of Prince Eugene and Marlborough combined, the allied sick and wounded were to be sent back to forward hospitals established in Donauwörth, before going on to Nördlingen. The hospitals for the French and Bavarians were brought forward to Dillingen on the Danube when their army had crossed over to confront Eugene on 10 August. This arrangement would, however, collapse in the wake of defeat as the Comte de Merode-Westerloo made clear in his informative memoirs. He recalled finding some of his own wounded Walloon soldiers abandoned on the road leading back to the Rhine 'They were doomed to stay in Ulm [and so faced capture] ... I had stretchers made for them, engaged good surgeons, had their soup and bread cooked, and finally had them brought into quarters.'

In the aftermath of any pitched battle these things could be a nightmarish business, particularly for those on the losing side. Surprisingly, though, many wounded men (and a few women) suffered severe wounds and survived to tell the tale. Donald

McBane lay wounded outside Blindheim village for two days before he was found by his friends and taken for treatment, while Jemmy Campbell serving with Stair's Dragoons wrote of a brother officer that, 'Willie Primrose is shot through the body but we are hopeful he will recover.'

In Marlborough's army each regiment or battalion had a surgeon and a surgeon's mate, and their skills were put to use both during a battle and afterwards. The gathering in of wounded for treatment was a problem, and varyingly applied, as Donald McBane found as he waited for his friends to find him. The day after Blenheim 100 men were sent from each allied battalion to scour the battlefield to locate and bring in the wounded, but their fallen French and Bavarian opponents were left where they were to fend for themselves, mostly unsuccessfully once local peasants came scavenging. Mrs Christian Davies remembers that even the living and unwounded prisoners taken were stripped of almost all they had and some were left nearly naked.

FEMALE SOLDIERS

A number of adventurous females masqueraded as men to enlist in the armies of 1704, serving in the ranks and wielding a musket or sword. Perhaps the best known example in British service in that of the Irishwoman Mrs Christian (Kit) Davies who became the first female Chelsea Pensioner in 1719. Marie Mouron, a French girl, was enterprising enough to enlist in two regiments at the same time, happily pocketing the bounty for doing so. She escaped drastic punishment when her deception was uncovered by arguing successfully that she should not have been accepted by either recruiting party.

Who was Who at Blenheim?

Anhalt-Dessau, Leopold, Prince (1676–1747)
Prussian officer commanding the Imperial infantry under Prince Eugene. The 'Old Dessauer' of Frederick the Great's wars.

Blood, Colonel Holcroft (1668–1707)
Commanded Marlborough's artillery in the 1704 campaign. His notorious father attempted to steal the Crown Jewels from the Tower of London during Charles II's reign.

Cadogan, General William, 1st Earl (1665–1726)
Marlborough's indispensable quartermaster-general and chief of staff. Became the master-general of the Ordnance on the Duke's death.

Churchill, Lieutenant-General Charles (1656–1714)
Marlborough's younger brother and general of infantry.

Clerambault, Philippe de Pallnau, Marquis de (d.1704)
French infantry commander in Blindheim village.

Cutts, John, Lieutenant-General, 1st Baron of Gowran (1661–1707)
'The Salamander.' Commanded the British and German infantry assault on Blindheim. Died in relative poverty while commander-in-chief in Ireland.

D'Arco, Count Jean
Piedmontese officer in Bavarian service. Commanded at the defence of the Schellenberg, and the Bavarian cavalry at Blenheim.

De la Colonie, Colonel Jean-Martin
French officer in the Bavarian service. Commanded the Grenadiers Rouge at the Schellenberg and defence of Rain.

Goor, Major-General John Wigand van (1647–1704)
Talented Dutch engineer officer. Killed leading the assault on the Schellenberg.

Hompesch, Graf Reynard Vincent van (1660–1733)
Accomplished Dutch cavalry commander, who fought in all Marlborough's major battles.

Lumley, Lieutenant-General Henry (1660–1722)
British cavalry commander in the 1704 campaign, and in all Marlborough's subsequent campaigns.

Maffei, Alessandro, Marquis de (1662–1750)
Italian major-general in Bavarian service. Fought as d'Arco's second in command at the Schellenberg, and conducted a skilful defence of Lutzingen village at Blenheim. Taken prisoner at Ramillies in 1706.

Natzmer, Major-General Dubislaw (1654–1739)
Prussian cavalry commander defeated with Count von Styrum at Höchstädt in 1703, and taken prisoner at Blenheim. Subsequently fought at Oudenarde (1708) and Malplaquet (1709).

Orkney, Lieutenant-General George Hamilton, 1st Earl (1666–1737)
Robust British infantry commander in the 1704 campaign. Fought at Ramillies (1706) and Malplaquet and became Governor of Virginia.

Parke, Colonel Daniel (killed in a riot, 1713)
Virginian rake and volunteer on Marlborough's staff. Wounded at the Schellenberg, and took the Blenheim despatch back to London in eight days.

Württemberg, Karl-Alexander, Duke of (1661–1741)
Commanded the Danish troops in allied service in all Marlborough's major battles.

Zurlauben, Beat-Jacques de la Tour Chatillon, Comte de von (1661–1704)

Highly capable Swiss cavalry officer in the French service. Commanded the gendarmerie of the French right wing at Blenheim and was mortally wounded.

John Marshall Deane, 1st English Foot Guards

The author of a valuable and detailed account of Marlborough's campaigns, John Deane served as a 'private gentleman centinelle' in the guards, and recounted his exploits and experiences as one of the Duke's faithful soldiers between 1704 and 1711. He was clearly an educated man, with a flair for telling a good story although he commendably did not embellish with overly lurid details in his otherwise accurate accounts, which were apparently written for the benefit of an acquaintance, perhaps a family member or influential patron, back in England. His access to quite detailed information on dates, marches and unit strengths indicates that he was perhaps employed as a clerk at Marlborough's headquarters, which is very possible, as the guards routinely provided the close protection for that organisation when on campaign. The daily camp bulletin that was issued would also, of course, have provided much additional detail. Dr David Chandler edited *A Journal of Marlborough's Campaigns [by] John Marshall Deane* in 1984, and provided an erudite and valuable introduction to these highly informative description of campaign life during the War for Spain, as it was fought in Flanders and southern Germany.

THE WEEKS
BEFORE THE BATTLE

The French and Bavarian threat to Vienna

Although Maximilien Wittelsbach, the Elector of Bavaria, owed allegiance to Emperor Leopold I of Austria, he had chosen to ally himself to King Louis XIV of France. In part, this was to safeguard his position as governor-general of the Spanish Netherlands, which he could clearly only hold with French blessing, but there was also a strong self-serving desire to be on the winning side in the war, and for much of the previous three years the French alone had seemed to hold the initiative. The Austrian war effort was hampered by a lack of money, military failure in the Tyrol and northern Italy, and distractions of rebellion in Hungary. In September 1703, an Imperial army had been soundly defeated by Marshal Villars at Höchstädt beside the Danube, although the French commander found it impossible to work harmoniously with the Elector, and Marshal Marsin soon took his place. The Imperial field commander in Swabia and Württemberg, Louis-Guillaume, the Margrave of Baden, proved incapable of countering the joint French and Bavarian operations, or of preventing fresh supplies and reinforcements from crossing the Rhine from Alsace and passing through the Black Forest to sustain the Elector. The free city of Ulm fell to the French, the security of Vienna itself was increasingly under threat, and it seemed that Austria was steadily being driven out of the war.

At its fullest extent, the strategic intention of the Duke of Marlborough, therefore, was threefold. Firstly, he would detach his troops from the Dutch and move south to combine with the imperial forces to protect Vienna; in this way the future of the Grand Alliance would be assured. Secondly, by shifting the strategic balance of the war away from the Low Countries to the Danube, he would seize the initiative and force the French commanders there to operate at full stretch, distant from their own depots and fortresses and with tenuous lines of supply and communication leading back through difficult country and across the Rhine. Thirdly, and perhaps most significantly, he would be free of Dutch caution and to a large degree could operate just as he saw fit. The difficulty was that he would still have to work with allies to whom he was at present unknown,

A British soldier gathers in captured French colours and kettle drums. (From the tapestry in Blenheim Palace. By kind permission of His Grace the Duke of Marlborough)

and his own lines of supply and communication would also be lengthy although depots were being established for his army in central Germany, and these were fairly free of the danger of French interference. An additional concern for the Duke was that parliament in London had not been fully consulted over this ambitious enterprise, and their army would in time be operating deep in southern Germany, seemingly very remote from British interests. They would be hostile if anything went badly wrong, and should he return to England as a defeated general, the risk Marlborough was taking was significant, both to his reputation and personally.

Marlborough had declared the intention to campaign on the Moselle to both soothe the anxiety of the Dutch and also that of parliament, but this was no mere cynical ruse. The Duke had no way of foreseeing a great and successful campaign leading to outright and historically resounding victory in open battle all the way off in southern Germany. He kept three distinct and promising possibilities in mind as the march up the Rhine began – to strike at the French forces commanded by General Bedmar in the Moselle valley, to attack the French army under Marshal Tallard in Alsace, or to go to Bavaria to confront the Elector and Marshal Marsin. All these were viable options open to him. Crucially, such a range of options were not available to his opponents, and the degree of the Duke's early strategic advantage can be seen in that light. The French, and to a lesser extent, their Bavarian allies, were reduced to reacting to what Marlborough did, from the start he set the pace and dictated the course of the campaign. However, matters would soon impel the Duke to discount the first two options and take his troops all the way to the Danube, and most notable of these events was the success of Louis XIV in sending reinforcements for the French army operating in Bavaria to the degree that the Imperial commanders would not be able to hold their own against them. This news of thousands of fresh French troops making their way through passes of the Black Forest came to Marlborough only four days after the march up the Rhine began. Briefly then, the French appeared to have taken away the Duke's freedom of movement, almost at the outset of the campaign, but he would prove to be light enough on his feet, and mentally nimble enough, to have made arrangements for just such an eventuality and his move southwards proceeded without a pause and, if anything, with greater urgency.

The Great March up the Rhine

On 4 May 1704, the British troops in garrison in Breda began their march to the concentration area set for Marlborough's army at Bedburg, near to Cologne. Charles Churchill, the Duke's younger brother and his general of infantry, took command four days later, with regiments from other garrisons joining the column as it progressed. A Grand Review of the army was held by Marlborough, and on 19 May the 19,000 troops began their march along the west bank of the Rhine. The region they passed through was all in allied hands, thanks to Marlborough's success in clearing out French garrisons over the previous two years. The route to be taken was well planned and prepared in advance, with marching in easy stages and supplies and replenishments ready at regular intervals on the road. That the troops were going through friendly territory, with local rulers either hostile to France, owing allegiance to the Emperor in Vienna, or already hiring troops for service to the Grand Alliance, was a great advantage, as was the ability of Marlborough's commissaries to pay for their supplies in hard cash rather than worthless scraps of promissory notes or outright confiscation. Francis Hare, serving on Marlborough's staff, remembered that 'His Grace was not unmindful to provide money and order regular payments for everything that was brought to the camp, a thing unknown hitherto.'

Hendrik of Nassau, Veldt-Marshal Overkirk, remained in command of the Dutch troops to safeguard southern Holland, and his early concerns at the wisdom of the whole project were put to rest as he saw that, as Marlborough marched south, the

French troops were also drawn away to match that movement. Louis XIV's commander in the Low Countries, Marshal Villeroi, could do nothing else or he would be outflanked by the Duke's marching army and could offer no assistance to the Marquis de Bedmar who commanded the French troops in the Moselle valley if he came under attack. The Duke held the initiative, and his opponents were reduced to responding to his moves; they were fixed in military terms. At this point they could not be sure of Marlborough's objective, which might well be to strike at Bedmar on the Moselle, or against French fortresses in Alsace – that the intention was to campaign on the Danube was still an unlikely prospect; possible, but surely doubtful given the risks to be run and the distance to be travelled. However, Marshal Tallard was taking a large reinforcement of troops, money and supplies through the Black Forest to reinforce Marsin in Bavaria, and would soon elude Baron Thungen's efforts to intercept him on the return to France – a neat military operation that was very well handled. Whatever Marlborough was doing, it remained clear that the French attempt with their Bavarian ally to strike decisively against Vienna was Louis XIV's main strategic aim at this point. The Duke might still strike on the Moselle or even in Alsace, but any such attempt would be unlikely to relieve the pressure on Vienna in good time. For the time-being however, French commanders had to deploy their troops to cater for such possibilities, and when it became clear that the threat had passed by in any particular locality, it was too late to attempt to regain the initiative as the Duke and his army marched onwards and out of reach.

The weather was fine as Marlborough's marching soldiers made their way southwards – 'over the hills and far away' as the soldiers sang – and they were joined at intervals by contingents of Hanoverian and Prussian troops, reaching Coblenz at the confluence of the Rhine and the Moselle on 26 May. Substantial supplies had been gathered there ready for the coming campaign, but instead of turning to attack the French in the Moselle, exposed as they were, the allied army crossed the

Rhine on pontoon bridges the next day and Villeroi, trailing along in Marlborough's wake, wrote to Versailles to report that 'There will be no campaign on the Moselle this year, the English have all gone up into Germany'. Marlborough now had pontoon bridges ostentatiously laid across the Rhine at Philipsburgh, indicating that he would strike at Alsace, and so the French were kept guessing as to his true intentions. Marching past Heidelberg, the army pressed on through deteriorating wet weather to Wiesloch and the Neckar River was crossed at Ladenburg, where a substantial reinforcement of Hessian troops joined the army.

Captain Robert Parker of the Royal Irish Regiment wrote approvingly of the arrangements for the troops as they toiled along the roads leading to Bavaria:

> We frequently marched three, sometimes four, days, successively, and halted a day. We generally began our march about three in the morning, proceeded about four leagues, or four-and-a-half each day, and reached our [camp] ground about nine [in the morning] ... Surely never was such a march carried on with more order and regularity, and with less fatigue both to man and horse.

The rain caused delays with the movement of the allied artillery and baggage 'The ill-weather with the badness of the roads for the artillery will keep the foot back for three or four days longer than I expected,' the Duke wrote early in June. Even so, Marlborough had clearly succeeded in safely detaching his army from their involvement in the Low Countries and in the process dramatically shifting the strategic balance of the whole war without the slightest interference from the French. Had the Duke's opponents just once realised his true intentions, they might have fallen on his field train of artillery, engineer stores and baggage labouring along increasingly muddy roads, and by doing so drag his whole operation to a halt far from his bases and dangerously isolated. Bewildered in the face of the captain-general's daring move, and full of concerns, this the French failed to do, and Marshal Marsin and the Elector of Bavaria, far from menacing Vienna and the whole future of the Grand Alliance, were faced with being isolated on the Danube. Marshal Tallard wrote to Versailles from Alsace 'In view of the superiority of the enemy forces between the Rhine and the Danube, assistance to Bavaria is so difficult.' Marlborough now admitted to the states-general that his firm intention now was to go to the Danube, but the Dutch remained calm, as they too could see that the French had been drawn away to the south, and they confirmed that the Duke could use Johan van Goor's corps of Dutch troops as he saw fit in the campaign. The French response was that Louis XIV sent fresh instructions that Tallard should take his army back through the Black Forest to reinforce Marsin and the Elector on the Danube. Marshal Villeroi, meanwhile, was to cover the early stage of the movement but otherwise to remain in Alsace, to ensure that the imperial and Dutch troops on the upper Rhine did not themselves move eastwards to join Marlborough.

Marlborough, Baden and Prince Eugene Combine

The small village of Mundelheim was reached by Marlborough on 10 June 1704, and there he first met Prince Eugene of Savoy. The president of the Imperial War Council in Vienna was a renowned field commander, who had campaigned with great success against the Ottoman armies in Eastern Europe. Eugene came to Mundelheim with Count Wratislaw to confer with Marlborough and the two commanders struck up an immediate and close friendship – the prince reviewed Marlborough's cavalry on 11 June and complimented the Duke on their fine condition after such a journey. So well had the march been organised, over poor roads and in deteriorating weather, that only some 900 men fell out through desertion or sickness, and many of the latter rejoined the ranks after some rest. The Margrave of Baden, courageous, obstinate, proud and prickly as he was, joined them at the Inn of the Golden Fleece at the village of Gross Heppach three days later, so that the allied commanders could agree on the future course of the campaign. There was some concern that Baden was corresponding indiscreetly with his old friend and campaign comrade the Elector of Bavaria, but he outlined a perfectly sound plan for the coming campaign – he and the Duke, once reinforced with Danish regiments who were still on the march, would manoeuvre to engage and defeat the French and Bavarian armies on the Danube, while Eugene went to the upper Rhine with his own Imperial troops and those of van Goor, to prevent another French reinforcement of their army in Bavaria.

On 17 June, Eugene went off to the defensive lines of Stollhofen on the Rhine, and Marlborough wrote to London of his plans to operate with Baden 'It being agreed that we act in conjunction for ten or twelve days, till the next of the troops come up [the Danes]'. The Margrave's Imperial troops secured the narrow pass over the Swabian Jura mountains at Geislingen, and Marlborough's army passed safely through, free from any interference from the Elector of Bavaria or Marshal Marsin. On 22 June, Marlborough, now reinforced by the Danish troops under the Duke of Württemberg, combined forces with Baden at Launsheim just a few miles to the north of the city of Ulm the Danube. The Duke's achievement was significant, for he had marched his British troops over 250 miles in thirty-five days from the Low Countries, reinforced and re-supplied en-route at regular intervals, and without interference from his opponents. Once the rear elements of his army closed up the force that he and Baden commanded would comprise over 60,000 men, and they could outmatch anything that the Elector and Marsin, with only some 45,000 troops, could at present bring against them. As such, a major shift in the strategic balance of the war had been accomplished, and the whole French strategy in southern Germany was in peril. Much now depended on the safe arrival on the Danube of a fresh French army under command of Marshal Tallard, and whether he could shake off the attentions of Prince Eugene while on the march.

The French and Bavarian commanders were well aware that they were for the time being outnumbered, although they could manoeuvre to use the obstacle of the Danube river to shield themselves, and they prudently fell back to assume a defensive posture in an entrenched camp at Dillingen, while further assistance was summoned from France. Marlborough had no heavy artillery, not having been able to bring the large pieces on the march from the Low Countries, and Baden failed to provide any despite assurances that he would do so; in consequence, the camp at Dillingen could not be attacked with any real hope of success. An observer wrote that, 'My Lord Marlborough has joined the troops under Prince Louis of Baden not far from Ulm, and the success of this affair will either gain him a great reputation, and very much shelter him from his enemies, or be his ruin'. Early in July, as the combined allied army prepared to move forward, news came in to the camp that Marshal Tallard had managed to evade Prince Eugene at the Lines of Stollhofen, and was now marching through the Black Forest with a fresh French army to join the campaign in Bavaria. The whole campaign was finely balanced, and if Marlborough and Baden did not force the line of the Danube now, they might not ever do so.

The Hill of the Bell

Marlborough needed to establish a forward base if he was to operate effectively south of the Danube. Depots that had been established in Franconia and central Germany were secure from French interference, but his present base at Nördlingen was too far to the north once the line of the river was crossed. The small town of Donauwörth, sitting neatly at the confluence of the Wornitz river and the Danube, would be very suitable for this, with a good bridge across the Danube, easily defensible from attack from the south, and with large storehouses ready for use. The importance of the place was obvious, however, and was firmly in the hands of his opponents, and the steep and partly wooded Schellenberg hill nearby was being fortified by a strong corps of Bavarian and French troops under the command of the very capable Piedmontese officer, Comte Jean d'Arco. 'Some 13,000 of the enemy were encamped upon the Schellenberg and they were very busy fortifying and entrenching themselves.' The hill had been fortified by King Gustavus Adolphus during the Thirty Years' War of the previous century, and d'Arco's troops were busily improving these now dilapidated earth-work defences. Understanding that he would soon be reinforced by the Elector of Bavaria, who would have troops on the march from Dillingen to support d'Arco, as soon as the threat to Donauwörth was appreciated, Marlborough decided on an immediate attack on the hill. With almost no pause, the marching troops were set on the road leading to the crossing over the Wornitz, at the small village of Ebermergen just a few miles to the north of the Schellenberg.

The custom was that the two commanders, Marlborough and Baden, held the command of the allied forces on alternate days – honour was, in this way, held to be satisfied. This was simply a

The old stone bridge at Ebermergen. Marlborough's troops crossed the River Wornitz here, on the march to attack the French and Bavarians on the Schellenberg, 2 July 1704.

diplomatic nicety in the interest of harmony, and to acknowledge Baden's own standing as an Imperial field commander of repute. In practice little more was involved than setting the password for the day, and Marlborough held the actual command, having most troops at hand, and it was he that drove the pace of the campaign forward. The Margrave was used to campaigning in a measured way, and was reluctant to make any frontal attack on the Schellenberg in what seemed to be such haste, feeling quite rightly that heavy casualties would result, but Marlborough could see that any delay would simply allow d'Arco the time to make his position more strong. The Duke was also spurred on in his decision by the news that Tallard was on the march, and so the operation went ahead, and Baden, to his credit, fully co-operated despite his reservations at the wisdom of what was planned. The attack was bound to be a stiff test, for the hill could only easily be approached on a narrow frontage, set as it was between the Wornitz river to the west and the broken and wooded ground of the Boschberg to the east; the chance for the allies to manoeuvre the defenders out of position was not available.

Marlborough had 130 men selected from each of his forty-five infantry battalions – grenadiers and volunteers – to form a powerful attacking force some 5,850 strong. These troops would act as the stormers for the assault on the hill, and in addition Lord John Mordaunt was appointed to command a 'forlorn hope' of eighty men picked from the 1st English Foot Guards. In immediate support were two 'divisions' commanded by Major-General Henry Withers and Count Gustav Horn, drawn from the leading elements of the army, and each comprising eight battalions of British, Dutch, Hessian and Hanoverian troops, about another 12,000 men in all. A third attacking echelon was formed of thirty-five squadrons of British and Dutch cavalry and dragoons, led by Major-General Henry Lumley and Graf Reynard van Hompesch. The narrow frontage on which the advance would be made did not allow Baden to deploy his wing of the army fully, but he agreed to provide a brigade of imperial grenadiers (two Swabian battalions and one Austrian) to support the attack. Colonel Holcroft Blood would place a large battery in position near to the small hamlet of Berg just to the north of Donauwörth, and the Margrave would also provide guns for the preparatory bombardment of the hill. In all, the allied commanders were able to deploy about 22,000 men and sixteen artillery pieces in the assault, in effect they formed the steel tip of the army's long march all the way from the Low Countries.

The allied soldiers moved forward from their encampment in the early hours of 2 July 1704 and despite the muddy roads they were across the Wornitz river at Ebermergen by mid–afternoon that day, using an old stone bridge and pontoon bridges laid in the adjacent meadows. Their advance was apparently not immediately detected by the French and Bavarians, but Marlborough was seen coming forward with a small party of officers to view for himself the preparations for defence on the Schellenberg. Count d'Arco had been at lunch with Colonel DuBordet, the French garrison commander in Donauwörth, but on learning of the allied approach he hurried to join his men on the hill, and to complete the preparations for the defence. He also had the cottages and houses in the outlying hamlet of Berg set alight, to try and delay

THE DEAD MAN'S WAGE

In Marlborough's army there was the enlightened practice of carrying a non-existent 'dead man' on the muster roll of each squadron or company, and the pay drawn for this phantom would be used for the relief of widows and orphans of the regiment. Although having no official standing, the practice was approved by Queen Anne as there was no formal system for the payment of pensions or compensation for disabling wounds. An alternative use for the expression was when volunteers for some hazardous task would pool the bounty money offered and divide it up amongst the survivors after the action. In this way it was said that 'they took the dead man's wage and the price of their blood.'

the deployment of his opponent's advancing troops. Christian Davies, the redoubtable female soldier serving as a dragoon in Marlborough's army, wrote that:

> Our vanguard did not come in sight of the enemy entrenchments 'til the mid-afternoon ... The duke ordered the Dutch General Goor who commanded the right wing, comprised of English and Dutch with some auxiliary troops, to attack as soon as possible. Thus we did not stay for the coming up of the imperialists (Baden's troops).

Just after 6 p.m. that evening, the two allied batteries near to Berg opened fire on d'Arco's men in their still incomplete defences, and straight away heavy casualties were suffered by the more exposed troops on the higher ground, who gained little protection from the forward breastworks. A French officer, Colonel de la Colonie, wrote that, 'The enemy's battery opened fire and raked us through and through'. Meanwhile the attackers were toiling forward up the steep slope, each man clutching a bundle of sticks, fascines, with which to bridge any obstacle they encountered. These were mostly wasted by being thrown into a sunken cart track on the lower slopes, and the troops pressed on upwards across the slopes towards the breastworks. D'Arco's guns could not depress sufficiently to fire into the dead ground used by the allied soldiers in their approach, but as they came up into sight they were swept by a ferocious hail of well-directed musketry and canister from the defenders at the breastworks. Scores of the attackers were quickly shot down, and Major-General van Goor, leading the assault on foot, was amongst those who fell, shot through the eye and dying soon afterwards. The forlorn hope pressed forward with great gallantry, the men shouting and cheering with all their might, and Colonel Munden, who went in with them, remembered that his new hat was all shot to pieces with musket balls. Despite overcrowding on the lower slopes, the assault was resolutely pressed forward and musket-butt blows and bayonet thrusts

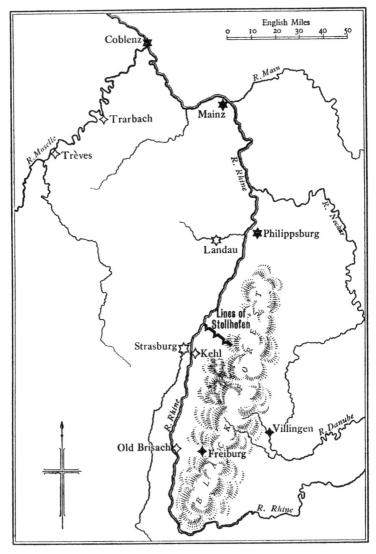

After the resounding success at Blenheim in August 1704, Marlborough found that the advance across the Rhine, and the autumn campaign in Alsace and the River Moselle, made slow progress.

were soon being exchanged across the breastworks. Casualties amongst the attackers mounted alarmingly, and Count von Styrum dismounted to lead forward and encourage a fresh wave of attackers, but he was soon shot down too, and the defence on the hill appeared to be as solid as could be. Marlborough, seeing that the troops were faltering in the face of such a fierce and well-directed resistance, moved forward his squadrons of cavalry to the foot of the hill, where they would be well placed to mount an immediate pursuit once the defences were carried, but also to deter the assault troops from falling back too rapidly and perhaps making off to a place of greater safety. 'The first line of Horse and Dragoons moved up, and stood so close, and animated the Foot so much by their brave example, that they rallied and went on again. The Horse were now, however, so near a mark for the enemy's shot, that a great many fell or were disabled.' The Duke also had Lord John Hay's Regiment of Dragoons dismount, and move forward to add their weight to the attack.

While this desperate hand-to-hand struggle went on, a frontal attack that showed every sign of failing, the Margrave of Baden led his detachment of Imperial grenadiers to the line of the marshy Kaibach stream that runs along the foot of the Schellenberg between the hill and the town of Donauwörth. This watercourse was in dead ground to d'Arco and his commanders on the steep slopes above, and Baden's progress around the left flank of the defenders on the hill was undetected for some time. The French Nectancourt Régiment, that had been posted to hold this part secure, had been drawn into the defences of Donauwörth by DuBordet, and as a result a gap in the French and Bavarian dispositions yawned open. As the grey-coated grenadiers turned to the left and began their climb, relatively untroubled by a scattering of shots from the town, the French commander of the Grenadiers Rouge, Colonel de la Colonie, recalled that, 'They arrived within gunshot of our flank at about seven thirty in the evening, without our being aware of the possibility of such a thing, so occupied were we in the defence of our own particular post.'

D'Arco, suddenly alerted to the danger to his flank, hurried to bring forward his reserve of dismounted dragoons from the rear of the hill, but these were shouldered aside by Baden's men, and the Comte found himself cut off from his own troops by the advancing grenadiers. His second in command, Comte Alessandro Maffei, attempted to draw some troops away from the defence of the breastwork to counter the new threat, but the defence rapidly fell into confusion under the weight of the combined allied attack on both the front and flank of the position. The French and

A Prussian dragoon, c. 1704. The dark blue coat with turnback regimental facings was typical of the Prussian troops. Moustaches were popular among German troops, but the British were usually clean-shaven.

Bavarian soldiers, who had fought very well, began to fall back, tormented by musketry from Baden's grenadiers on their flank, and with the British, Dutch and German troops pouring over the now abandoned breastwork what began as a limited withdrawal quickly became a rout. As Marlborough sent his cavalry and dragoons over the slopes in ruthless pursuit, the beaten troops were in headlong flight in the rainy evening. They were chased and harried down to the banks of the Danube, where a pontoon bridge erected the previous day collapsed under the weight of fleeing men crowding across, and many of the fugitive soldiers were drowned in the fast-flowing waters.

This was a complete victory for Marlborough and Baden, although gained at a startlingly heavy cost. Some 1,400 allied soldiers were killed and another 4,000 wounded that evening, including the Margrave who had been shot with a musket ball in the foot. Of Mordaunt's forlorn hope of eighty men only seventeen survived the day unhurt, and valuable officers such as van Goor and Styrum lay amongst the dead strewn all across the slopes. Of the 12,000 or so French and Bavarian defenders of the Schellenberg, at least 2,000 unwounded prisoners were taken, and only some 3,000 others (d'Arco and Maffei among them) ever rallied to rejoin the Elector's army south of the Danube. This was a heavy blow, as the defenders on the Schellenberg had been amongst the best regiments available and they could not easily be replaced. Donauwörth had to be abandoned the next day, and the Bavarian pontoon train left behind for the allies to use, and an attempt by DuBordet to fire the magazines and supply depots in the town was thwarted by the citizenry. The Colonel also failed to properly destroy the bridge over the river.

Marlborough now had both his forward base and a crossing point over the Danube ready to pursue a campaign in Bavaria. Better still, three days after the battle was fought long-awaited Danish reinforcements, twenty-one cavalry squadrons and seven battalions of infantry, joined Marlborough and encamped that night on the Schellenberg. On 3 July 1704, Marlborough was able to write with quiet satisfaction to Queen Anne, announcing the first success of his campaign in the Danube:

> I most humbly presume to inform Your Majesty that the success of our first attack of the enemy has been equal to the justice of the cause Your Majesty has so graciously espoused. Mr Secretary [Robert] Harley will have the honour to lay the relation of yesterday's action before you. To which I shall crave leave to add, that our success is in great measure owing to the particular blessing of God, and the unparalleled bravery of your troops.

There was inevitably some criticism in parliament at the heavy casualties sustained, but Marlborough was now close to achieving his principal aim in marching south from the Low Countries. His army, and that of Baden, was free to move across the Danube and

Marlborough's great cavalry charge to break Tallard's army, on the evening of 13 August 1704.

interpose itself between the French and Bavarians and Vienna. The outposts at Ingolstadt and Rain were isolated and could be picked off, while the fighting capability of the Elector was significantly weakened by his losses in the catastrophic defence of the hill above Donauwörth. Emperor Leopold was in no doubt about what had been achieved and he wrote in warm terms to the Duke with his thanks and congratulations:

> My generals and ministers declare that the success of that enterprise (which is more acceptable and advantageous to me, in this present time, than almost anything else that could befall me) is chiefly owing to your councils, prudence, and execution, and the wonderful bravery and constancy of the troops, who fought under your command. This will be an eternal trophy to your most serene Queen in upper Germany, whither the victorious arms of the English nation have never penetrated since the memory of man.

After such a resounding defeat for some of his best troops, it was hoped that the Elector of Bavaria might be inclined to abandon his alliance with the French, but this proved to be a false hope. Despite the shock he had suffered, the Elector remained obstinate, drew in his scattered garrisons, and fell back southwards from his entrenched camp at Dillingen to a more secure position behind the river Lech near to Augsburg. He did however, send envoys to Marlborough and Baden to discuss a possible cessation of operations, but this was soon found to be just a ploy to gain time while French reinforcements drew nearer. Marlborough and Baden had hopes that Eugene could still interrupt or seriously delay Tallard's progress, and the Duke wrote on 9 July: 'We have heard nothing of Prince Eugene since the 5th, so that we take it for granted that the Marshal de Tallard has not pursued his march, which he began on the 2nd of this month'. He was mistaken; the fresh French army was still coming on to campaign on the Danube and combine with the now beleaguered forces of Marsin and the Elector.

THE GRENADIERS ROUGE

This regiment in the Bavarian service comprised French and Italian deserters, criminals and other miscreants, who volunteered to serve in the ranks of what was almost a penal battalion to avoid their punishment, which would probably entail going to the galleys. Despite the roughness of the raw material recruited in this way, the men of the Grenadiers Rouge proved to be sturdy fighters, commanded by Colonel Jean-Martin De La Colonie, who left informative memoirs of their service at the Schellebnberg fight in July 1704.

That same day, Marlborough's cavalry crossed the Lech at Gunderkingen to lay siege to the French and Bavarian garrison in the small town of Rain, but operating so far forward of his established bases continued to pose difficulties. 'Now we have met with a disappointment,' the Duke wrote to a friend in London, 'in the want of our artillery from Nuremberg for attacking Rain, wherein the enemy have a garrison of about a thousand men, which we are unwilling to leave behind'. Despite the lack of heavy guns, the siege was successfully concluded eight days later, and on 18 July Marlborough could close his main force up to the Lech and in doing so placed himself firmly between the French and Bavarian army and Vienna. The initial aim of his whole campaign was achieved – unless Marsin and the Elector came out of their defences to fight in the open, or there was some inexplicable error on the allied side, the Emperor in Vienna was safe.

That much was achieved, but Marlborough could not keep his army in Bavaria through the winter and into the following year and a decision had to be forced. Frustrated at the prevarication of the Elector, the Duke let loose his cavalry and dragoons on 25 July to devastate the rich farming country between the Danube and Munich. 'We are going to burn and destroy the Elector's country,' he wrote, 'to oblige him to hearken to terms.' For miles around,

Bavarian farms, villages and hamlets were put to the torch, crops destroyed and flocks and herds seized in a ruthless campaign of destruction. 'The allies sent parties on every hand to ravage the country,' Christian Davies remembered, 'who pillaged above fifty villages, burnt the houses of peasants and gentlemen, and forced the inhabitants with what few cattle had escaped to seek refuge in the woods'. Marlborough's aim in this brutal act of war was twofold – firstly he hoped to force the Elector to come to terms, and secondly, if he would not do so, then Bavaria was to be ruined as a base from which any army could easily operate through the coming months. The Margrave of Baden, inclined to a more measured way of campaigning and alarmed at the scale of destruction being caused, protested to the Duke, but Marlborough ignored him. 'Our whole business,' he wrote to the secretary of state in London, 'has been to burn and destroy the Elector's country ... [he] can expect nothing less than the ruin of Bavaria for his obstinacy.' Even if the allies could not force things to a conclusion that summer and had to march away, the French would be unable to maintain themselves on the Danube, to perhaps try to re-impose the threat to Vienna, other than at enormous effort with supplies having to be brought through from France. This campaign of destruction was that of the grim reality of warfare, of cruel necessity, and gave the Duke no pleasure, writing to his wife that:

> My nature suffers when I see so many fine places burnt, and that must be burnt ... This is contrar to my nature, that nothing but absolute necessity could have obliged me to consent to it, for these poor people suffer for their master's ambition. There having been no war in this country for above sixty years.

Prince Eugene, however, was not at all impressed with the progress that Marlborough and Baden were making, writing that, 'They amuse themselves laying siege to Rain and burning a few villages instead, according to my opinion, which I have made known to them clearly enough, of advancing directly upon the enemy'.

Tallard, meanwhile, having evaded Eugene's attentions, was all this time making his way to the Danube with his army. Marshal Villeroi had covered the initial movement across the Rhine very well and decoyed Prince Eugene away from Tallard's line of march at a critical moment, but had then retired to stand guard over Alsace, apparently unaware that the allied covering force was also on the move. Tallard then spent several days attempting in vain to seize the minor Imperial fortress of Villingen, not far from the hilly headwaters of the Danube, but he moved on when Eugene approached. As was their custom, the French troops foraged, confiscated and scavenged on the route, and encountered fierce opposition in the unfortunate districts through which they passed. Having delivered supplies to the magazines and storehouses in Ulm, on 6 August the Marshal joined forces with Marsin and the Elector at Biberbach on the Lech not far from Augsburg. Their combined army now numbered some 56,000 men and 90 guns, even though the Elector had diverted many troops to protect his own estates from Marlborough's cavalry raids. Marsin was particularly scathing at this wasteful dispersion of some of

EATING UP A COUNTRY

A ruthless practice in warfare at the start of the eighteenth century was to have an army live off the land and literally 'eat up a country' before moving on and leaving a near-wasteland behind. The strategic advantage of this was that an opponent could not then subsist his own army in that region; this was a method used quite often by French commanders. War is a cruel business and the local population would inevitably suffer, resisting such activities as far a possible, so the clear advantages to a commander were uncertain. The devastation of Bavaria by Marlborough's cavalry and dragoons in the weeks before Blenheim was of a similar brutal nature, but with a different purpose: the Duke hoping to force the Elector to come to terms rather than fighting on.

the best Bavarian units, writing to Versailles that, 'The Elector has thirty-five good battalions and forty-three squadrons of good troops, of which since the entry of the enemy into Bavaria he has had only twenty-three squadrons and five battalions with the army'. As always, coalition warfare is a tricky business, and in any case it seemed that orders had been given that the Elector's private estates were not to be harried. The Elector was persuaded by Tallard to recall those regiments dispersed in places such as Augsburg and Memmingen, but they would not all be able to join the main army in time.

Prince Eugene had shadowed Tallard's march, but had not enough strength to seriously impede his progress. The same day that the French and Bavarian forces combined at Biberbach, Eugene reached the Plain of Höchstädt on the northern bank of the Danube, and he rode over to confer with Marlborough and Baden at Schrobenhausen just to the south of Donauwörth. The Allies still had superiority in numbers, although Eugene's small army was rather exposed north of the Danube. It was soon agreed that the Margrave should take his 16,000 imperial troops (twenty-three battalions and thirty-one squadrons) to attack the Bavarian-held fortress of Ingolstadt further down the Danube, while Marlborough and the prince remained to confront the French and Bavarians, even though by dividing their forces in this way the allied commanders were giving up a distinct numerical advantage. This was a serious consideration, and while a detachment of imperial cavalry, 800 strong, had already been sent to invest the fortress, with Baden gone they would be able to deploy only some 52,000 troops and 60 guns, rather fewer than their opponents. It is at least possible that the Marlborough and Eugene preferred to have the cautious and possibly obstructive Margrave out of the way during the series of aggressive movements that were about to be undertaken, although possession of Ingolstadt would certainly be a prize well worth having, clearing the line of the Danube from Höchstädt eastwards, especially if an early decision in the campaign could not be forced. The line of the river would be firmly in allied hands, and they would be able to draw on the depots and magazines established in central Germany, while their opponents were left in a ruined land, devoid of ready supplies.

Although not yet aware that Baden was making for Ingolstadt, the French and Bavarian commanders now felt confident enough to try and strike at one of the two detachments of the allied army while they were still apart, with Eugene's troops camped at Höchstädt to the west of Donauwörth, and Marlborough still south of the Danube between Exheim and Rain, at least a good day's march away. The Duke was in something of a dilemma, and could not yet move to join Eugene north of the river until he was sure that his opponents had done so, otherwise he might expose Baden's detachment at Ingolstadt to attack. If, on the other hand, Eugene came south of the river prematurely, then the allied lines of communication and supply northwards to Nördlingen and Nuremberg might be exposed. As it was, Marsin and the Elector preferred to push the pace of the campaign, even though the more cautious Tallard would have preferred them to bide their time and wait for further reinforcement from France and, perhaps, to allow Marlborough's ambitious and increasingly over-extended campaign to wither away in the cold months of the autumn. After a somewhat heated discussion, it was at last agreed to try and attack Eugene, and on 10 August, the day after Baden began to march eastwards to begin the siege at Ingolstadt, the French and Bavarian armies began to cross to the north bank of the Danube over pontoon bridges laid at Dillingen. Prince Eugene, with only about 20,000 troops, was now in real danger, unless the allied armies could quickly complete their concentration. The move was soon detected, however, and he immediately wrote to the Duke with an urgent summons heavy with significance and notable for bringing on one of the great battles in history:

> The enemy have marched. It is almost certain that the whole army is passing the Danube at Lauingen. They have pushed

a Lieutenant-Colonel that I have sent to reconnoitre back to Höchstädt. The Plain of Dillingen is crowded with troops. I have held on here all day, but with [only] eighteen battalions I dare not risk staying the night. I quit however with much regret [the position] being good and if he takes it, it will cost us much to get it back. I am therefore marching the infantry and part of the cavalry this night to a camp I have marked out before Donauwörth. I shall stay here as long as I can [...] Everything, Milord, consists in speed and that you put yourself forthwith in movement to join me tomorrow.

Eugene, having prudently sent his infantry marching to take up a depth position at Donauwörth, remained to bar the road, with twenty-two squadrons of cavalry and dragoons on the line of the Kessel stream just to the west of the town. If attacked, he could fall back on his supports and in the process close the gap with Marlborough's approaching army. The Duke, however, needed no urging and he had promptly moved an advanced detachment of twenty-seven squadrons of cavalry and dragoons under the command of the Duke of Württemberg to reinforce Eugene. Charles Churchill was sent with twenty infantry battalions hurrying to the north bank of the Danube as additional support. Despite having to cross three rivers – the Lech, the Danube and the Wornitz – the marching troops made good time. Eugene called forward his infantry once more, and on Monday 11 August, the two allied armies combined successfully at Münster on the Kessel, nearly a full week after their opponents had done so. A moment of acute danger for their whole campaign had passed safely by, and that evening at about 6 p.m., Marlborough and Eugene met on the road just outside the village, and could hold their crucial council of war.

For the French and Bavarians, however, it seemed that they had out-manoeuvred their opponents – they had combined their own armies and had a slight numerical advantage now that Baden was known to have marched away to Ingolstadt with his troops. The initiative in the campaign seemed to lie with them, as the season for good campaigning was speeding by with Marlborough not best placed to force a decision before he would have to take his army either to winter quarters in central Germany, or perhaps all the way back to the Low Countries. Such complacency was highly dangerous, for Eugene's precautionary movement to the eastwards had drawn them on from Dillingen, and out onto the now vacant four-mile wide Plain of Höchstädt, still thick with ungathered harvest of the coming months. This was a convenient place to encamp their army, but also a good place to fight a battle, unlike the more marshy ground of the Pulver and Brunnen streams around the nearby village of Höchstädt itself. With two such dangerous opponents in close proximity, it was essential that Tallard, Marsin and the Elector remained vigilant, and yet they were so taken up with the illusion of their own successful manoeuvring that they remained blind to the danger that they had, in effect, been brought out into the open to fight. 'By this march of the Elector and the two Marshals,' Marlborough's Camp Bulletin read, 'they entirely abandon the country of Bavaria, having nothing left there but the garrisons of Munich and Augsburg'. There was, of course, no mention of what was to happen next.

THE BATTLE OF BLENHEIM:
Wednesday 13 August 1704

Preparations for the Battle

The French and Bavarian army was comfortably encamped on the Plain of Höchstädt, taking advantage of the ground along the Nebel and Maulweyer streams, between the villages of Blindheim (Blenheim) on the banks of the Danube, Oberglau, and Lutzingen against the wooded hills of the Jura to the north. The marshy streams that cut across the plain were an obstacle to easy movement, and would serve to delay any approaching opponent, but the French Marshals and the Elector apparently had few concerns that they would be attacked in place. A French officer, the Marquis de Montigny-Langost, wrote that these streams had partly dried up in the warm summer weather, being only 'two feet in width, which formed a small marsh which greatly deceived our generals,' and Tallard did suggest that the Nebel be dammed to make it more difficult to cross, with gun emplacements prepared for artillery. The Elector refused to allow this as he did not want to damage the still unharvested crops on the plain any more than was necessary, and in any case there was no real expectation of having to fight a battle there so the trouble did not seem worthwhile.

13 August

7.30am	allied approach to Plain of Hochstadt seen from the Franco-Bavarian camp
11.00am	Franco-Bavarian deployment complete - artillery bombardment begins
12.00 noon	Eugene in position to attack in combination with Marlborough
12.30pm	allied attack begins all along the line of battle
3.00pm	allied infantry attacks repulsed at Blindheim, Oberglau and Lutzingen
4.00pm	Marlbrough's main cavalry attack begins on Tallard's squadrons
5.00pm	French counter-attacks repulsed, second attack by Marlborough begins
6.00pm	Marlborough's cavalry begin to overwhelm Tallard's horsemen
7.30pm	Tallard's squadrons break and flee. Tallard is captured
	Marlborough writes the Blenheim Despatch
	Fresh attacks begin on Blindheim village
	Marsin and the Elector begin to withdraw
9.00pm	French garrison in Blindheim surrender
21 August	News of the victory at Blenheim reaches London

The Comte de Merode-Westerloo, a highly opinionated Walloon cavalry officer in the service of the French claimant to the throne of Spain, wrote:

Our right wing was on the left bank of the river Danube with the village of Blindheim some two hundred paces to its front [...] The Elector and his men held a position stretching as far as Lutzingen, which contained his headquarters, with the wood stretching away to Nordlingen to his front. All in all this position was pretty fair.

The senior officers and their staffs installed themselves in the barns and cottages of the small villages dotted about the plain, Tallard in Blindheim, Marsin in Oberglau, and the Elector in Lutzingen, and the tents of the army were laid out in neat lines, while the well-ordered routine of encampment took its comforting course. However, in their fatal false sense of security, the French and Bavarian commanders had neglected to station troops some

Eugène-Jean-Philippe, Comte de Mérode-Westerloo, commander of a brigade of Walloon cavalry at Blenheim and author of some very entertaining memoirs. He viewed the allied deployment for battle from his camp bed.

1,000 metres or so to their front, where the small hamlet of Schwenningen lay in a narrow gap less than a mile wide, set between the Danube and the wooded slopes of the Fuchsberg hill to the north. This was a terrible oversight, explained only by their conviction that they would not have to fight there at all, for had this simple precaution been taken, with just a couple of good battalions of French infantry in Schwenningen, their position on the wide Plain of Höchstädt would have been almost impossible to approach by the allied troops except at the cost of heavy fighting and a total loss of the element of surprise.

By the afternoon of Tuesday 12 August 1704, Marlborough and Eugene had begun moving their army westwards from their own encampment at Münster. The ground was well known to the Prince, although not to Marlborough, and a final reconnaissance was carried out by the two men from the church tower at Tapfheim and a small hill near to Wolperstetten, from where a good view of the French and Bavarian camp was to be had. Pioneers were busy clearing the wooded paths beside the road leading westwards, and all this activity could not be entirely concealed, especially as they had some 52,000 men and 60 guns on the move close behind. The Duc d'Humieres, a French cavalry commander whose troops

Cottages in Blindheim village, opposite the churchyard, which were in existence at the time of the battle.

were out gathering forage nearby, was curious enough to send a detachment forward to find out what was going on, but these squadrons, commanded by the Marquis de Silly, were driven off by the brigade of British infantry commanded by Archibald Rowe as they approached to take possession of the gap at Schwenningen.

Rowe's troops, together with the 1st English Foot Guards and Wilkes's Hessian brigade, occupied that small hamlet with little difficulty, and the narrow approaches to the Plain of Höchstädt were in this way neatly secured by nightfall. The lively Comte de Merode-Westerloo tried to take part in the skirmishing and remembered: 'I rode out beyond Blindheim village into the corn-filled plain, taking care not to stray too far from my escort which I might well have needed. When I saw our troops falling back, I also returned to camp.' That the suspicions of the French and their Bavarian comrades was not at all aroused by this activity is surprising, but Tallard that same evening was writing to his King in Versailles, to say that prisoners taken during the recent encounters had reported that the allied army was expected to withdraw from the campaign and retire into winter quarters. 'Rumour in the country expects them at Nordlingen,' he wrote. Whether this mis-information was planted deliberately, as is sometimes reported, is actually unclear. Marsin afterwards claimed that, 'We called a Council of War to consider whether we should stay for the enemy, who was marching towards us.' If this was so, rather than the Marshal just making excuses after the event, then their neglect in appreciating the true allied intentions, or doing anything about holding the gap at Schwenningen, is all the more remarkable.

After enjoying a good bowl of campaign soup with his officers that evening, Merode-Westerloo remembered that, 'I don't believe that I ever slept sounder than on that night,' but the French and Bavarian commanders at all levels had clearly miscalculated the daring intentions of Marlborough and Eugene to a considerable degree. The allied army lay on its arms in the wooded hills that night, while their opponents remained comfortably in their tents on the nearby Plain of Höchstädt, blithely unaware of the imminent

Tapfheim church. Marlborough and Eugene viewed the French and Bavarian encampment from the church tower on 12 August 1704.

threat that they faced. In the early hours of 13 August, the allied troops were roused from their rough bivouacs, and fell quietly into line by tap of drum, moving out onto the tracks and road leading towards the Schwenningen defile, which had been secured by Archibald Rowe since the previous evening. Marlborough took the opportunity to discuss the terrain with Major-General Dubislaw Natzmer, who had fought and been defeated by Marshal Villars at Höchstädt the previous September, and as a grim result knew the ground well. 'Whilst viewing the features of the enemy's position at a short distance,' Francis Hare wrote, 'His Grace was also more particularly informed of the nature of them by Major-General Natzmer, of the King of Prussia's troops, who had been wounded the year before in the defeat at this place.' He added that, 'The morning being a little hazy, the enemy might suppose that we had only small parties abroad, and might not be aware that the whole army was in motion [...] They remained quietly in their camp during the early part of the morning.' Even so, and with so much achieved by their daring march, the immediate and daunting task

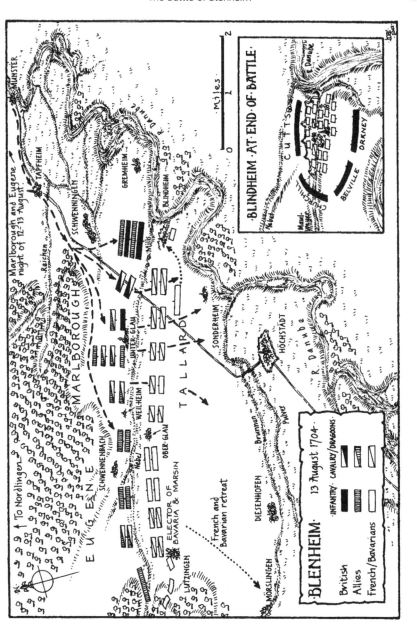

89

that the allied commanders faced was to thread their army through the narrow defile and deploy ready for battle onto the wide plain without interference from the French and Bavarians who had the advantage of already being in place. If they took action quickly enough, and moved forward to challenge the allied deployment, then they might cause chaos amongst the marching columns. That the approach of the allied army was a complete surprise is clear, as orders had been given for foragers to go out that morning as usual.

Meanwhile, Merode-Westerloo, lying snugly in his camp bed in a barn near to Blindheim, was hurriedly woken by his gesticulating groom who 'blurted out that the enemy was there ... flinging wide as he spoke the doors of the barn and drawing my bed-curtains. The door opened onto the fine, sunlit plain – and the whole area appeared to be covered by enemy squadrons. I rubbed my eyes in disbelief.' The Comte dressed hurriedly, swallowed his morning cup of hot chocolate, and began rousing his troops to ready themselves for battle, while signal guns were fired to recall the foragers and piquets – the reports of the opening guns could be heard by the Margrave of Baden forty miles away at Ingolstadt. Meanwhile, hurrying to the church tower in Blindheim, Tallard, Marsin and the Elector could see the columns of the allied army swarming through the Schwenningen defile and rather than marching away to the north, were instead deploying for battle. It was clear that the three commanders, in their neglect, had been caught completely by surprise.

Marlborough wrote in his report the day after the battle: 'We marched between three and four yesterday morning [...] About six we came in view of them enemy, who we found did not expect so early a visit.' So much had been achieved by daring and all to the good; however, it would take some time for the allied army to be ready to mount a serious attack, and this should enable a robust defence to be prepared along the line of the Nebel stream – all was not yet lost for the French and Bavarian commanders by any means. Prince Eugene with his 20,000 troops and 20 guns had the hardest task, having to make his way across difficult

The church tower in Blindheim village. The French and Bavarian commanders viewed the allied deployment form here on the morning of 13 August 1704. The walled churchyard was the scene of savage fighting.

gently rising ground to take up a position on the allied right, ready to attack Oberglau and Lutzingen. Meanwhile, Marlborough with 32,000 men and 40 guns had a simpler and shorter route to take to get into place along the Nebel stream near the hamlet of Unterglau and facing the village of Blindheim on the left of the allied line. Their task would, however, be made easier by the way in which the French and Bavarians had gone into camp, administratively convenient, but not ideal when having to deploy and fight a battle there.

The marshy Nebel, although rather drier than normal as noted by Montigny-Langost, provided a useful barrier to easy movement. The Elector of Bavaria would fight his own battle around Lutzingen, on the left of the line, with his own flank shielded by infantry posted in the wooded hills to the north, but the two French Marshals could not agree on what course was best. Marsin chose to move his troops close to the streams around Oberglau to make any attempt by the allied troops to get across an expensive business. Tallard, however, was keen to make use of his cavalry on the open plain beside Blindheim, and preferred to allow his opponents to come over the Nebel before fully engaging them; in this way the allied commanders would be drawn on to fight

The Duke of Marlborough directs the Battle of Blenheim. (From the tapestry in Blenheim Palace. By kind permission of His Grace the Duke of Marlborough)

with a water obstacle at their back – always a risky thing to do and courting disaster if things went wrong and a hasty withdrawal became necessary. So, each of the two French commanders went their own separate way to engage the enemy as they saw fit; both men were correct after a fashion, but this lack of co-ordination was not a promising start to a day which had seen such dangerous opponents as Marlborough and Eugene close up to them without their true intentions being detected.

To their credit, the French and Bavarian commanders quickly recovered from the shock of the unexpected allied approach, and they arranged their troops for the coming battle with energy and competent skill. The hamlet of Unterglau and nearby Weilheim Farm were set alight to hamper the approaching allied troops, as were two water mills on the stream near to Blindheim. The villages of Lutzingen, Oberglau and Blindheim were barricaded and prepared for defence, and Tallard had twelve squadrons of dismounted dragoons deployed in a position from the marshy banks of the Danube to Blindheim, which initially had a garrison of just nine battalions of French infantry. Four more battalions stood to the rear, ready to move forward to support the garrison, and these should have been ample to keep the place secure. Three more battalions, from the elite Régiment du Roi, were stationed at the side of the cottages and gardens, linking the defenders of the village with Tallard's main force of thirty battalions, who gave support to the cavalry on the plain. Marshal Marsin could deploy fourteen French and émigré Irish battalions to hold the small village of Oberglau, supported by two more battalions sent across by Tallard, while another twelve French battalions held the line stretching towards Lutzingen. That village was garrisoned by nine Bavarian battalions in their distinctive red stockings under the command of Comte Alessandro Maffei, and a further eleven French battalions were stationed in the woods beyond the cottages to hold the left flank of the whole line secure.

The French artillery, commanded by the very capable Marquis de Frequeliere, was hauled into place to sweep the Nebel stream with fire, although the uncut crops and the slope leading down from the plain made good observation tricky in places, while a large Bavarian battery was established on the outskirts of Lutzingen, enjoying a good field of view across the stream towards the hamlet of Schwennenbach. The gunners in Lutzingen and Oberglau could achieve an overlapping cross-fire, making any advance against either village a murderous business. This cross-fire could not be achieved between Oberglau and Blindheim, partly due to the greater distance between the two places, but also to the curve of the slope leading up onto the Plain of Höchstädt. Tallard's sixty-four squadrons of French and Walloon cavalry, although reduced in numbers by sickness amongst the animals, were drawn up in impressive order on the wide open cornfields to the side of Blindheim, ready to move forward in counter-attack at the right moment. Marsin and the Elector had forty French and twenty-seven Bavarian squadrons of cavalry to support the

Blindheim village and church tower seen from the edge of the River Danube. The extreme right of Tallard's position was held here by dismounted French dragoons.

infantry from Oberglau and Lutzingen, while sixteen squadrons were posted to give support to Tallard's left flank. By late morning, as the deployment of the allies slowly progressed, the Elector and his fellow commanders could feel that, after the initial surprise, they had recovered their tactical poise rather well, and were quite ready for whatever might come.

Although Marlborough got his forty-four battalions of British, German and Dutch infantry into place fairly quickly along the line of the Nebel, supported by eighty-two squadrons of cavalry, Eugene's progress towards Lutzingen and the left of the enemy battle-line was more troubled. The gently rising ground that he had to cross with his eighteen Prussian and Danish battalions and seventy-nine squadrons of cavalry and dragoons was broken, and the farm tracks rutted and uneven, and he had to throw out flank guards to the left in case Marsin should dart forward from the area around Oberglau to challenge his deployment. No such threat developed, but the Prince was delayed in the process, and as the hours of the morning went by it seemed that the precious advantage so daringly seized was being allowed to drift away. Francis Hare remembered that, 'The ground upon the right being found less practicable than it had been represented to be, Prince Eugene was forced to make a greater circuit through the woods upon his right, and to extend his wing further than had been anticipated'. In the meantime, Tallard's artillery had begun to bombard Marlborough's troops as they closed up to the Nebel, on either side of the smoking ruins of Unterglau, and began their preparations on the banks of the stream to allow them to cross the obstacle without too much delay. 'About eight o'clock, the enemy began to cannonade our army as it advanced. Upon which His Grace ordered Colonel Blood to plant several batteries upon the most advantageous parts of the ground,' Hare wrote. A French round-shot struck the ground beneath Marlborough's horse at one point, covering rider and mount with dust. The Duke calmly ordered that the men should lie down to gain some protection from both the French gunnery and from the hot August sun while

The Duke of Marlborough and his quartermaster-general William Cadogan. A 'running footman' can be seen behind the Duke, ready to set off at Marlborough's command. (From the tapestry in Blenheim Palace. By kind permission of his Grace the Duke of Marlborough)

they waited for Eugene to get into place. 'All the while the armies cannonaded each other very briskly,' Francis Hare went on, 'but the fire of the enemy's artillery was not so well answered by the cannon of Prince Eugene as it was by that of the left wing, for his highness was obliged to sustain the fire of the enemy's artillery all the while he was drawing up his troops, but could not bring his own pieces to bear against them'.'

Eugene was, of course, having trouble getting his troops into place, and the cumbersome guns were making heavy going of getting over the difficult ground around Weilheim Farm. Fascines were brought forward to bridge the ditches and streams in the area but 'his cannon were kept in the meantime at too great a distance to reach those of the enemy with effect'. The exchanges of artillery fire grew in intensity as the gunners bedded their pieces in and got the range and casualties began to mount on both sides. Merode-Westerloo remembered: 'I was riding past Forsac's Regiment when a shot carried away the head of my horse'. The Comte was soon remounted by his groom, but he would lose twelve more horses during the course of the hectic day.

Given the apparent strength of the French and Bavarian dispositions, and the time that had unavoidably been allowed them to prepare their defences, some of Marlborough's generals doubted that a successful engagement could even be made. 'Almost all the generals were against my Lord's attacking,' Hare recalled, and even the normally aggressive George Hamilton, 1st Earl of Orkney, wrote afterwards that, 'Had I been asked to give my opinion, I had been against it, considering the ground where

Armour

The use of armour for personal protection had largely died out by the Blenheim campaign, except in those few Cuirassier regiments still in the service of Austria and Bavaria. The expense of equipping an armoured horseman, and the weight of the armour itself, made their employment less flexible, and even the simple breastplates of the 'ordinary' allied regiments of horse were put away into store by Marlborough. The front-part of the breastplates were, however, re-issued in 1707. Some soldiers wore a 'secrett', an iron skullcap, under their hat to ward off sword slashes, but these were hot and uncomfortable, and were not widely used.

they had been camped and the strength of their army. But his Grace knew the necessity there was of a battle.' As it was, having come so far and achieved so much, there could be no backing down or second thoughts now for the allied commanders. In the event that they had tried to retire or to perhaps manoeuvre for a better opportunity, there was little prospect that they could march their troops back through the narrow Schwenningen defile or the wooded hills behind them without the French and Bavarians pursuing and turning the withdrawal into a rout. The allied army

George Hamilton, 1st Earl Orkney, Marlborough's aggressive infantry commander and subsequently the governor of Virginia.

had, by the daring approach march, taken up a position from which it was almost impossible to withdraw in good order; so, a battle it had to be, and any lack of major success would place Marlborough and Eugene in real peril. 'I know the danger,' the Duke had written, 'yet a battle is absolutely necessary'. The critical moment was approaching, and Merode-Westerloo recalled the scene at midday: 'It would be impossible to imagine a more magnificent spectacle. The two armies in full battle array were so close to one another that they exchanged fanfares of trumpet calls and rolls of kettle-drums.'

The Battle Begins – the Assault on Blindheim Village

Divine Service had already been read at the head of each allied regiment, and no doubt the French and Bavarians were also imploring the Almighty to give them success that day. Shortly after midday, some six hours after the allied army threaded its way through the Schwenningen defile, a galloper came to Marlborough with word from Prince Eugene that even though all his artillery was not yet in place, he was ready to go into the attack on Lutzingen and Oberglau. The Duke sent a message back that he should do so forthwith, and had the troops were called to their feet, dressing and alignment checked, and at last they moved forward to cross the Nebel stream. 'It was one o'clock before the battle began,' Marlborough wrote. On the left of the allied line, Lord John Cutts' column of the British brigades of Rowe and Ferguson, and the Hessians under Wilkes, moved steadily across the gentle slope towards the barricaded village of Blindheim, close alongside the banks of the Danube. The preparations for the defence of the village had been well carried out, with footbridges thrown across the small Maulweyer stream that ran amongst the cottages to allow rapid movement of troops from one part to the other as the allied threat developed. All the entrances had been barricaded with barn doors, carts, and furniture and chests dragged out from the larger properties, whose walls were loop-holed for musketry.

Lord John Cutts of Gowran was nicknamed 'the Salamander' for enjoying the hottest fire. He commanded the British and German attack on Blindheim village. He died in Ireland in 1707 while commander-in-chief there.

Harried by canister fire from French guns on the nearby slope, the British troops neared the cottages and were swept with a fierce and disciplined musketry from the French defenders from the Régiments de Navarre, Artois and Greder Allemagne, and Archibald Rowe was shot and killed at the head of his brigade, as were two of his officers who ran to help him. Lieutenant-Colonel Philip Dormer of the 1st English Foot Guards was also mortally wounded as they advanced against the Régiment de Provence, while Ferguson's brigade quickly found that they could not drive the dismounted French dragoons from the makeshift defences leading down to the river-bank. As the British troops fell back from the village to recover their order, a smart counter-attack was sent forward by Major-General Beat-Jacques von Zurlauben, with three squadrons of the elite French Gens d'Armes sweeping down from the Plain of Höchstädt to cut in at the exposed flank of Rowe's own regiment which was thrown into confusion as it hurriedly tried to form square to receive the mounted charge. William Primrose, the Colour Ensign, was hacked down and the Colonel's Colour seized by a triumphant gendarme. 'The French Gens d'Armes,' Hare wrote, 'fell upon the right flank of Rowe's brigade, put it partially in disorder, and took one of the Colours of Rowe's regiment.'

Wilkes's Hessians had now crossed the Nebel and rose from the marshy grass alongside the stream; at this dangerous moment, with the right flank of Cutts's whole column under threat, they moved smartly forward to help the stricken British infantry. Their disciplined volleys of musketry, described as 'a peal of fire which obliged them to make more haste back', drove the French cavalry away with some empty saddles, and the lost Colour was dropped and recovered by Rowe's regiment as it reformed its battered ranks. The Gens d'Armes retired a short distance and re-ordered their slightly ragged ranks, while von Zurlauben called forward more of his squadrons ready for a fresh effort. In the meantime, Cutts was able to send his British and Hessian brigades into the attack on the village once more, with hand-to-hand fighting across the barricades, but the French defence remained resolute and the attackers were once more thrown back. The effect of these hard-pressed assaults, however, was significant. The French commander in Blindheim, Philippe de Pallnau, Marquis de Clerambault, had been entrusted to defend the place 'to the last extremity' by Tallard, and he became increasingly anxious at the security of the place, beginning to draw in those nearby infantry battalions that were intended to support the French cavalry on the open plain. By late-afternoon, no fewer than twenty-seven battalions of infantry and twelve squadrons of dismounted dragoons were packed into the close confines of the village and the adjacent gardens and

The Plain of Höchstädt, looking westwards towards Lutzingen. Prince Eugene's cavalry attacked across this ground.

The Plain of Höchstädt from the rear of the French positions, looking across the French and Bavarian deployment.

orchards. Many of these 12,000 troops had no field of fire at all, and so were unable to properly participate in the fighting, while the French cavalry had been stripped of much of the support it needed to operate effectively. Captain Robert Parker of the Royal Irish Regiment recalled of the French troops in Blindheim that: 'They had not the room to draw up in any manner of order, or even make use of their arms'. By then Marlborough had sent a message to Cutts to make no more of these expensive attacks, but just to secure the left of the allied line, and hold the French infantry in the crowded village for as long as possible. With no more than about 8,000 of his own troops under command, and some of those soon pulled away to the fighting on the plain itself, Cutts achieved this key task admirably well, and held the right of the French line firmly in his grip.

Prince Eugene's Attack

While the fighting for Blindheim went on, Prince Eugene sent his imperial and Prussian squadrons, under command of Prince Maximilian of Hanover, to pick their way across the broken rivulets of the Nebel and engage Count von Wolframsdorf's Bavarian cavalry on the cornfields between Unterglau and Lutzingen. The marshy obstacle here was apparently more difficult than downstream but their attack was initially successful in pushing back Wolframsdorf's foremost squadrons. This success could not be sustained and the second line Bavarian squadrons came forward with French support and resolutely drove Maximilien's troopers back. At the same time, the eleven Prussian and seven Danish infantry battalions, under the robust command of Prince Leopold of Anhalt-Dessau, moved to attack the Bavarian and French defenders of Lutzingen: 'He showed no regard for danger, and did lead on his followers most courageously'. The lines of infantry went forward into a heavy artillery fire from the batteries placed around the village, and at heavy cost Finck's Russian Brigade forced their way at bayonet point into the gun positions, the soldiers of Margraf Ludwig's Regiment fighting hand to hand with the Bavarian gunners for possession of the artillery pieces. The Prussians were then driven out by a stinging counter-attack from the Bavarian infantry, led by two battalions of the Elector's Liebegarde Fusilier Regiment, and had to fall back to reform for a fresh effort. The Bavarians quickly manned their guns once more, and the ranks of Prussian infantry were shredded with heavy canister fire at murderously close range. Their position could not be maintained, and with their supporting cavalry being driven away on the left, they fell back to the Nebel, in the process uncovering the flank of the Danes who were already fiercely

Prince Leopold of Anhalt-Dessau commanded Prince Eugene's infantry in the attacks on Lutzingen, the 'Old Dessauer' of Frederick the Great's wars.

engaged with du Rozel's French infantry in the woods to the north of the village. Eugene's infantry scrambled back across the stream in some disorder. Losses had been heavy; several Prussian regimental colours were lost in the confusion, and it would be some time before the attack could be renewed with any prospect of success.

Marlborough recalled that: 'The Elector and M. Marsin were so advantageously posted that Prince Eugene could make no impression on them'. The Prince rode forward to rally the shaken troops, but a fresh attempt by his second-line imperial cavalry led forward by the Duke of Württemberg to force their way across the stream failed to make very much ground under the brutally effective cross-fire of artillery from Oberglau and Lutzingen. A sharp second counter-attack by the Elector's cavalry was, however, a rather half–hearted affair and was not pressed across the marshy stream in the way it might have been. Eugene's batteries were now hammering away from a good position near to Weilheim Farm, but a third advance by Eugene's re-formed cavalry failed to make any progress across the Nebel. Both sides were clearly tiring fast on the northern half of the battlefield, and another attack by Anhalt-Dessau's infantry at about 4.30 p.m. which inevitably lacked the spirit and energy of their first effort, could not make any impression on the defences of Lutzingen. Anhalt-Dessau exhorted his men onwards, waving a shot-torn Prussian regimental colour over his head, but men were falling fast on either hand, and even though they gained a toe-hold in the Bavarian battery once more, the defence of Lutzingen was as solid as ever. The French and Bavarians stood their ground, and with volleys of musketry beat the attack off once more with heavy losses, 'The Elector of Bavaria was seen riding up and down,' it was noted, 'and inspiring the men also with fresh courage'. Scholten's Danes also had to fall back on the right, the French Régiment de le Dauphin putting in a slashing counter-attack to restore the security of the left of their line. Prince Eugene had ridden over to add encouragement to the infantry assault, and in the press of the fighting a Bavarian dragoon levelled his musket at him, but was smartly bayoneted by a Danish soldier before he could fire. For all their local success in driving off this fresh attack, Maffei's troops were themselves too battered to pursue and make the most of their local success, and were unable to take the valuable chance to turn the second Danish and Prussian withdrawal into a rout at the muddy Nebel's edge. Both sides had clearly exhausted themselves on this part of the field; for the moment neither could attack the other with any real prospect of success, and the battle would now have to be decided on the Plain of Höchstädt.

Despite the smart rebuff that Eugene had suffered, and his severe casualties, the overall course of the day was taking shape as Marlborough had intended and sketched out in his mind as he rode to battle that morning. Heavy attacks had been thrown against both flanks of his opponents, and their attention was unavoidably focused on holding firmly to the villages of Blindheim on their right and Lutzingen on the left. Precious reserves of infantry had been devoted to these tasks, and Marsin and the Elector were fully occupied in holding off Eugene's attacks. All this while, Marlborough's main force made its careful way across the Nebel stream, almost unopposed apart from artillery harassment, and out onto the firm dry ground on the edge of the Plain of Höchstädt to confront

Emperor Leopold I of Austria. His field commanders had proved incapable of stopping the French and Bavarian campaign in 1704, until the arrival of the Duke of Marlborough.

*Camille d'Hostun,
Comte de Tallard.*

Tallard and his French cavalry. The Marshal had so far done nothing to stop Clerambault from packing infantry battalions into the confines of Blindheim, and his fine squadrons now lacked adequate support, although the true effect of this had yet to be seen. Marlborough, on the other hand, had managed to array his army on the open plain, carefully interlacing his eighty-two cavalry squadrons with infantry and guns for mutual support. He was even able to draw away from Lord Cutts on the left of the allied line the British brigade under Hamilton, and St Paul's Hanoverians together with the dismounted dragoons of Hay's and Ross's Regiments, to add their weight to General Charles Churchill's eighteen battalions of British, Dutch and Hessian infantry as they deployed onto the gentle slopes of the open plain.

The French artillery had been busy and managed to inflict some losses on Marlborough's troops, but these were not significant enough to hamper his deployment, and Major-General Henry Lumley had moved five squadrons of British cavalry under the command of Colonel Francis Palmes without too much difficulty to shield the open flank of Cutts' brigades as they faced Blindheim. A sudden second counter-attack was made by eight squadrons of the French Gens d'Armes to try and split Churchill's infantry away from Cutts. The moment was tense, for most of the allied horsemen were still composing themselves after their scrambled crossing of the stream. Palmes led his cavalry forward to meet the new threat, and as the French horsemen halted to fire off their pistols and carbines in the old outmoded style, he was able to envelop them by throwing out a squadron on each side of the French cavalrymen, and then drive them in confusion back on their supports. 'The English squadrons charged up to them sword in hand, and broke them and put them in flight.' A true and very neat tactical success, but Palmes then allowed his troopers to go too far in their pursuit, and they tired and were cut up by fresh French squadrons that came forward to support the Gens d'Armes. Harried by musketry from the nearby Régiment du Roi, Palmes got his cavalry back out of trouble in something of a scramble, with the support once more of Wilkes's robust Hessian infantry, but the effect of this cavalry skirmish, with probably no more than a few dozen casualties on either side, was quite significant.

The French in Disarray

This second repulse of the elite French Gens d'Armes was unsettling, and Marshal Tallard wrote afterwards in his report, trying rather lamely to explain his failure, that: 'Although there were eight squadrons on our side, the five enemy squadrons sustained their shock and made them recoil'. His attention was now firmly fixed on the re-ordering of his cavalry, perhaps explaining his neglect to rectify Clerambault's error in cramming Blindheim with infantry. The Elector of Bavaria, hearing of the rebuff to the Gens d'Armes and apparently unable to resist interfering, remarked to his aide-de-camp the Marquis de Montigny-Langost: 'What? The gentlemen of France fleeing? Go, tell them that I am here in person, rally them and lead them to the charge once again.' The young aide was sent galloping across the field, but he recalled being intercepted by allied horsemen: 'I received two cuts on the head, a sword thrust through the arm, a blow from a musket ball on the leg, and my horse was wounded.' The Marquis was then taken captive and relieved of his purse, but managed to get away in the smoke and confusion of the battle. While his wounds were being bandaged by his groom, he viewed with dismay the growing deployment of Marlborough's troops on the edge of the plain, apparently without being seriously challenged, and one of his comrades recalled that: 'We neglected the great double lines, which were forming at the foot of that fatal hill.' Von Zurlauben did lead his squadrons forward in another counter-attack, the Hanoverian cavalry regiments of Noyelles and Voigt taking the brunt of the charge and being pushed back towards the stream and potential defeat, but this effort was then driven off by well-directed musketry from the supporting allied troops. 'They had brought their infantry well forward, 'the Comte de Merode-Westerloo recalled, 'and they killed and wounded many of our horses.' The valiant von Zurlauben was among those who were wounded in the attempt, and he died two days later.

The Hanoverian dragoons commanded by Lieutenant-General von Bulow then pursued the Gens d'Armes as they fell back. In their enthusiasm they crossed the small Maulweyer stream that flows down towards Blindheim village, and then became entangled with the Régiment du Roi whose well-directed volleys of musketry once again threw the troopers into some confusion. The dragoons had to scramble back towards their own supports to recover their order. In growing concern at a tactical situation that suddenly seemed to be escalating out of control, Tallard sent to Marsin with an urgent request for reinforcements, but this was refused – Prince Eugene was clearly to be seen re-ordering his own troops across the stream and could well make a fresh attack at any time. Long lines of allied troops could even then be seen apparently readying to move forward to the Nebel opposite to Oberglau, while Eugene's artillery was firing in full force with the batteries emplaced between Schwennbach and the Welheim Farm pounding the defenders of Oberglau and the French squadrons in

Die Reuter und Dragoner

A cartoon of some rather campaign-weary cavalrymen and dragoons. French dragoons typically wore the stocking cap depicted here, but British dragoons wore the tricorne, like the regiments of horse.

the adjacent fields. Marsin had more than enough to deal with as it was, and Tallard had to fight on with what he had to hand.

In the centre of the field, the Duke of Württemberg led his Danish cavalry across the Nebel, but a smart counter-attack by Marsin's French squadrons drove them back over the stream to recover their order. Simultaneously, Count Horn's Dutch, Swiss and Prussian infantry forced their way forward to attack the Marquis de Blainville's French garrison in Oberglau, and so secured the right flank of Marlborough's advance against Tallard. Shortly after 3 p.m., the Prince of Holstein-Beck and Major-General Pallandt were directed to secure the village itself, but their Dutch troops were quickly thrown back by the émigré Irish regiments of Clare, Dorrington and Lee. The leading regiments of Goor and Beynheim were routed and dispersed, many being taken prisoner: 'So warmly received that after a sharp dispute they were forced to retire,' Francis Hare recalled. The Dutch infantry fought doggedly, but were driven away step by step in a bayonet-stabbing and musket-butt-wielding contest with the Irish. As his troops fell back in increasing disorder towards the marshy ground of the edge of the stream, Holstein-Beck sent a message to Count Fugger,

DRAGOONS AS CAVALRY

The original role of the dragoons was as mounted infantry, riding to battle or patrolling but then fighting on foot with musket and bayonet. Rates of pay were less for dragoons than for the troopers in the regiments of horse, and their smaller mounts were cheaper to buy than cavalry chargers, so their use in the mounted role, unsurprisingly, was growing. In time, British regiments of cavalry, the horse, would be re-mustered as dragoons to save money, but were given the title of 'Dragoon Guards' to avoid offending both officers and men.

standing near to the Weiheim Farm with a brigade of Imperial Swabian cuirassiers, calling for him to come urgently to support. The Count refused to move, as he had orders to anchor Eugene's flank at this point and would do no more without instructions; his reluctance to move was understandable, for his cuirassiers ensured the security of Eugene's left flank as his attacks drove in against Lutzingen. Holstein-Beck was wounded soon afterwards and taken prisoner by the French; although he was released later that day, he died soon afterwards and Count Berensdorf took over the command of his troops at a difficult moment.

Across the wide Plain of Höchstädt the contending armies were in close and bitter contest, and an observer wrote that: 'From one end of the armies to the other everyone was at grips and all fighting at once'. The success of the day still hung very much in the balance, and Marshal Marsin now had a fleeting chance to strike hard and split the allied army into two struggling halves, each of which would be unable to support the other and ready to be defeated in detail. The Marshal sent his twenty squadrons of French cavalry and dragoons cantering forward through the Irish infantry, who opened ranks to allow them through, against the exposed flank of Churchill's infantry deployed opposite to the smouldering ruins of Unterglau. Their rapid advance across the

Unterglau village, looking east across the Nebel stream. Marlborough's troops crossed the stream here to form up on the plain of Höchstädt.

marshy ground had disordered the ranks of the French horsemen, and a pause was necessary to recover their dressing before moving on. In the delay that resulted, Marlborough was able to divert St Paul's Hanoverian brigade to meet the threat, together with Erbach's brigade of Dutch cavalry and a battery of guns that Colonel Blood could swing round and bring to bear. 'The Duke of Marlborough,' Francis Hare wrote, 'seeing things in some confusion, galloped up, and ordered forward three battalions, commanded by Major-General Averock, to sustain them, and caused a battery of cannon to be brought forward, affairs were re-established at this point.' A new request was sent by the Duke to Count Fugger to move forward, and this time he complied promptly, bringing his armoured cuirassiers 'Moving closen liken to a brassen wall,' as it was remembered, across the sloping fields from Weilheim Farm. This imposing advance threatened Marsin's advancing troopers on the bridle hand, the weaker side away from the sword arm, and they halted and turned to meet the cuirassiers – the chance to strike with any real effect at Churchill's infantry passed, and in so doing so did the last moment of real peril for Marlborough and Eugene.

The Duke now directed Count Berensdorf with Dutch, Hessian and Hanoverian infantry to pin Marsin's troops to the defence of Oberglau, and this task was achieved in a bitterly fought struggle. The French commander there, the Marquis de Blainville, was amongst those mortally wounded, while leading soldiers from the Poitou Régiment in a desperate counter-attack. Meanwhile, Earl Orkney could press onward with the rest of his infantry onto the Plain of Höchstädt to provide Marlborough's cavalry with the close support they needed.

Merode-Westerloo commented ruefully that, once Marsin's own attack from the vicinity of Oberglau had stalled: 'They had given ground to the enemy who were pouring over the stream and forming up on my flank in the very midst of our army'. Having allowed the Duke to deploy his troops across the Nebel stream, Marshal Tallard had failed to deliver any telling attacks to disrupt the ordering of his cavalry, and these were now ready to launch their main attack. The Marshal's own horsemen were ragged and tired after the scrambling fights without adequate infantry support earlier in the day, but the bulk of Marlborough's squadrons, able when needed to draw on their infantry for assistance, were fresh and in good order. It was late afternoon and the shadows were beginning to lengthen. Marlborough could see that all was ready for the great stroke against the French cavalry that he had planned throughout the anxieties of the long, hot August day. With the bulk of the French and Bavarian infantry now devoted to the defence of the three villages, and held firmly in place, they were unable to have any real influence on the cavalry battle. Eugene was gallantly pinning the Elector of Bavaria against Lutzingen and the wooded hills to the north, while Marsin's troops were striving to hold onto Oberglau against the driving attacks of Berensdorf's infantry – there was no one now for Tallard to turn to for support at this critical point. Too many of his infantry battalions were caught up in Blindheim village and his cavalry were only supported by the nine small battalions of recently recruited French infantry, holding a position beside the road to Höchstädt. These young troops had advanced to assist in the withdrawal of the French Gens d'Armes after their encounter with Palmes and his British troopers, but had then come under a heavy fire from Blood's gunners and had fallen back to resume their former position, leaving a scattering of dead and wounded men behind them.

Marlborough's Great Attack

Francis Hare remembered that: 'The Duke of Marlborough had got the whole of the left wing of the allied army over the rivulet and our Horse were drawn up in two lines fronting that of the enemy, but they did not offer to charge till General Churchill had ranged his Foot also in two lines behind the cavalry.' The careful balance of cavalry and infantry, supported by artillery, was in place and all was ready for Marlborough to strike at the centre of gravity of the Franco-Bavarian army, Tallard's almost entirely unsupported squadrons of cavalry. 'About five o'clock the general forward movement was made, which determined the issue of this great battle, which until then had seemed to remain doubtful. The Duke of Marlborough, having ridden along the front, gave orders to sound the charge.' The Duke waved his commanders forward – Lieutenant-General Henry Lumley with the British and Prussian cavalry on the left and the Duke of Württemberg on the right with Hanoverian and Danish squadrons. The advance by some 8,000 allied horsemen across the open plain, at a steady trot so as not to tire the horses too soon, supported by some 14,000 infantry, was robustly met by the first-line French cavalry now commanded by the Marquis d'Humieres as von Zurlauben was lying gravely wounded. These squadrons valiantly pushed Marlborough's cavalry back onto their infantry supports, and Merode-Westerloo wrote that his squadrons 'charged and flung them back'. The allied troopers could fall back on their infantry while they recovered their order, and once again, the French were exposed to the lash of musketry, emptying many saddles. Hare recalled that the old and outmoded practice of firing pistols from the halt was still being employed by the French: 'Those of the enemy presented their fusils at some small distance and fired, but they had no sooner done so than they immediately turned about.' This was the correct drill to reload weapons, but such rearward movements could soon tumble out of control in the press and heat of a mounted action. Now, the fresh second-line allied squadrons, Hessians, Hanoverians, Saxons and Dutch, under command of Graf Reynard van Hompesch and the Count of Ost-Friese, fresh and in fine order, rode forward in full array and it was a battle-winning stroke. Captain Robert Parker remembered that: 'Our squadrons drove through the very centre of them, which put them to entire rout.'

The ordering of the first line French squadrons crumbled under the relentless allied pressure, and they rode to the rear to attempt to recover but instead disrupted the ranks of their second line that remained in support. The adjutant of the Gens d'Armes wrote afterwards in a letter to the French Minister for War that 'We had charged twice before the cavalry had approached the enemy, we faced them until six o'clock in the evening. It was in the centre which was thin and weak, where the enemy pierced through.' Disorder in the ranks of the French squadrons was spreading quickly and the troopers were increasingly looking over their shoulders, while shouted commands and drum rolls were disregarded. With the press of disciplined allied horsemen so close behind, panic quickly took hold, and whole squadrons of French cavalry lost their composure completely, turned about and attempted to ride headlong off the field. Then, Merode-Westerloo recalled:

There was a definite but unauthorised movement to the rear ... two musket balls killed my horse beneath me so that he subsided gently to the ground. One of my aides-de-camp and a groom came up with another horse after observing my fall, and they soon had me hoisted onto horseback again.

Meanwhile, abandoned by their cavalry, the nine battalions of young infantry still valiantly held their ground beside the Höchstädt road, only to be shot down in rank and file. Francis Hare wrote that:

Colonel Blood was ordered at the same time to march a battery over the pontoons [across the Nebel] and to bring it to bear on the enemy's battalions. This was done with good success and made a great slaughter of the enemy. They stood firm, however, for a time, closing their ranks as fast as they were broken, until being much weakened, they were at last thrown into disorder, when our squadrons falling upon them, they were cut down in entire ranks, and were seen so lying after the battle.

As the French cavalry collapsed, and turned to flee from the field, Merode-Westerloo's horse was born up by the press of panicked riders on either side so that the hooves did not touch the ground for some minutes, before Merode-Westerloo was thrown down a bank with many others and trampled on before being found and remounted once again by his faithful groom. A pontoon bridge across the Danube gave way, and some troopers attempted to swim their horses across the river in their urgent desire to escape, but most who tried were drowned in the fast-flowing waters. A last desperate attempt by the Marquis de Gruignan to pull together some squadrons of Gens d'Armes and mount a fresh counter-attack which was brushed aside, while Tallard sent the Marquis de Maisonelle galloping over to Blindheim to belatedly draw out some of the infantry there to support the cavalry, but the aide-de-camp was never seen again and was presumably killed on the way.

The Marshal now rode towards the village, but it was all too late and too little, and not far from the hamlet of Sonderheim he was accosted on the way by a party of Hanoverian dragoons commanded by Colonel Beinbourg. Tallard, whose son had just been killed at his side by a dragoon, was conducted to the Prince of Hesse-Cassell, and sent on to Marlborough, who was then directing the pursuit of the broken French squadrons.

In an elaborate exchange of courtesies between the two commanders, who were well known to each other, Marlborough welcomed the beaten marshal: 'I am very sorry that such a cruel misfortune should have fallen upon a soldier for whom I have the highest regard'. Tallard murmured in reply: 'I congratulate you on defeating the best soldiers in the world'. The Duke's pointed response was: 'Your Lordship, I presume, excepts those who had the honour to beat them?'. Intent on pressing his victory onwards, Marlborough then put Tallard into his own coach with other senior captives and provided them with refreshments. He then turned to an aide-de-camp and asked for some paper. The scrap that was to hand was a tavern bill from earlier in the campaign, but it served well enough to become the famous Blenheim Dispatch. Without comment, Marlborough dismounted and, taking a pencil, scribbled on the reverse of the bill a brief note to his wife, Duchess Sarah, in London:

> I have not time to say more but to beg you will give my duty to the Queen and let her know that her Army has had this day a glorious victory. M. Tallard and two other generals are in my coach and I am following the rest. The bearer, my aide de camp Colonel Parke, will give her an account of what has passed. I shall doe it in a day or two by another more at large.

Daniel Parke was no mean horseman, and eight days later the same note was in the hands of Queen Anne in Windsor Castle, and she learned in this way that, at her wish, her Captain-General had crushed one of Louis XIV's finest field armies on the banks of the Danube, and the world was changed forever.

Marlborough writing the Blenheim Dispatch, 13 August 1704. In fact, the Duke dismounted to do so. (Courtesy of Dr David Chandler)

The Blenheim Dispatch, written on the back of an old hotel bill, was sent by the Duke of Marlborough from the battlefield. *'I have not time to say more but to beg you will give my duty to the Queen, and let her know her Army has had a glorious victory.'*

On the field of battle, the triumph still had to be concluded – Tallard and his cavalry had been swept away but Marshal Marsin and the Elector of Bavaria were still doggedly holding onto their positions. Still, Count Scholten's Danish infantry were now steadily pushing the French infantry at point of bayonet out of the wooded hills to the north to outflank the defenders of Lutzingen, and Marlborough's advance would soon make the French hold on Oberglau untenable. If they held on they would be enveloped and destroyed in place. As the evening sped by, the two commanders, aware that some disaster had evidently befallen the right wing of the army, extricated their troops, fired the cottages in Lutzingen and Oberglau to slow any pursuit and began a well-ordered withdrawal, 'with great dexterity and expedition,' as Richard Kane remembered, towards Diessenhofen and Morselingen to the westwards. Graf Reynard van Hompesch was directed to disrupt this move with his cavalry, but in the failing light the French and Bavarians were mistaken for some of Eugene's advancing Imperial troops, and in the delay this caused they were able to get away without serious interference. Robert Parker recalled that Prince Eugene:

> Perceiving the squadrons under Hompesch coming down that way, he took them to be some of Tallard's squadrons drawing down to join the Elector, whereby he halted, lest they should fall on his flank. The Duke also seeing Prince Eugene's troops so near the rear of the Elector's army, took them to be a body of Bavarians, making good the Elector's retreat, and thereupon ordered Hompesch to halt.

Given the severity of the fighting, the casualties suffered and the general weariness of troops and commanders alike, this confusion is perhaps not surprising. Marlborough had now to devote his attention to the village of Blindheim, where the large French garrison was still firmly in possession.

The Final Act in Blindheim

The British and German infantry commanded by Lord Cutts attacked Blindheim once more, but still had not the strength to break in and seize the centre of the village, and so Earl Orkney directed Webb's British brigade and St Paul's Hanoverians to move back from the Plain of Höchstädt to add their weight to the renewed attack. 'As soon as General Churchill saw the defeat of the enemy's Horse, he sent to inform Lord Cutts that he was himself coming to attack the village of Blenheim in flank, and requested that his Lordship would make another attack at the same time in front.' The dismounted dragoons of Hay and Ross were also sent into the assault, cutting off any chance of a late withdrawal from the village, and in fierce and bitterly contested fighting the French were gradually pushed towards the walled churchyard. John Deane of the 1st English Foot Guards remembered that: 'We, according to command, fought our way into the village'. The French resisted with desperate bravery and progress was slow, so much so that Colonel Belville was sent with two battalions of Hanoverian (Celle) infantry to bolster the dragoons who were on the point of being driven back by a spirited counter-attack mounted by the Régiment de Artois led by Colonel de la Silviere.

The Marquis de Clerambault, whose folly in taking so many infantry into the village had done such damage, was nowhere to be seen. He was rumoured to have drowned in the Danube while trying to escape, although he may equally possibly have been lying amongst one of the piles of the dead that choked the narrow alleyways, swept as they were with allied musketry as they pressed forward through the orchards and gardens around the village. The repeated discharges of the muskets had set some of the roofs of the cottages alight, and others had been fired deliberately to slow the allied attackers – many wounded men who had sought shelter were now in danger. 'Many on both sides were burnt to death,' remembered John Deane, 'great and grevious were the cryes of the wounded and those suffering in the flames after we

Blindheim village churchyard and nearby barns. The French and British infantry fought a bitter battle for this strongpoint in the evening of 13 August 1704.

entered the village and none is able to express it but those that heard it'. Night was coming on, and it seemed that the French hold on the village would not be prised loose before darkness fell. Marlborough even sent word that the attacks should be suspended and renewed in the light of the next morning, while Tallard sent a message that he would order a ceasefire so that the French troops could retire from the field and avoid further bloodshed. The Duke's cool response to this was that the Marshal was to be reminded that, sitting in his captor's own coach, he now had no command at all.

Captain James Abercrombie, who served on Orkney's staff, wrote: 'My Lord Duke's Aide de Camp came and acquainted My Lord Orkney that His Grace had sent to inform him that he should lie upon his Arms that night and that he would join him in the morning'. Instead, Orkney decided to attempt to force a conclusion one last time. The Marquis de Denonville, who commanded the Régiment du Roi, had already been captured during the savage fighting around the churchyard. During a brief truce that was arranged to rescue some of the wounded men from the burning cottages, he and Colonel Belville was sent to confer with the Marquis de Blanzac, who, in the absence of Clerambault, had reluctantly taken on the doomed command in Blindheim. The Marquis was conducted to where Orkney stood at one of the French barricades in a narrow street littered with the dead and wounded of both armies, and they told the astonished Frenchman that Marshal Tallard was already a captive. They insisted that further resistance was futile but that the attack must be renewed unless the garrison submitted without delay. Permitted to go to the edge of the village to confirm how things on the plain lay for himself, and unaware of the lack of numbers that he faced, de Blanzac was reluctantly persuaded of the futility of further resistance. As darkness fell, some 10,000 French infantrymen, among them the very finest of Louis XIV's regiments, were commanded to lay down their arms and colours and surrender the village. 'Salamander' Cutts, who still stood with his weary infantry on the trampled grass between the Nebel and the outlying cottages, expressed himself to be amazed at the capitulation given the strength of the defences. The simple fact was that the French infantry had not been overcome, but had been abandoned by their senior commanders and those left had suffered a collapse in command and morale. A more robust commander might well have negotiated better terms, perhaps even safe passage off the field, for the numerous and still dangerous garrison.

As it was, with the submission of the troops in Blindheim, Marlborough's victory over Tallard's army was complete and he could write the next day to the secretary of state in London: 'Let me know Her Majesty's pleasure relating to M. De Tallard and the other general officers, as for the disposal of near 1,200 other officers, and between 8,000 and 9,000 common soldiers, who being all made prisoners by Her Majesty's troops are entirely at her disposal.' The Duke, cautious as he always was with money, added: 'As the charge of subsisting these officers and men must be very great, I presume Her Majesty will be inclined that they be exchanged for any other [allied] prisoners that offer. I

Mrs Christian (Kit) Davies. Born in Ireland, she served with Hay's Dragoons throughout the Danube campaign of 1704 and was wounded at Ramillies two years later. She became the first female Chelsea Pensioner.

should likewise be glad to receive Her Majesty's directions for the disposal of the standards and colours ... there cannot be less than a hundred.'

At the end of a long, tiring and dangerous day, the victors could rest. The allied troops, too weary and battered to pursue their beaten opponents very strongly, camped on the field, and took advantage of the vast haul of gear that had been abandoned. These included: '100 fat oxen, ready skinned [...] welcome booty to the soldiers,' according to Francis Hare. Mrs Christian Davies remembered that: 'I was one of those detached to guard the prisoners, and surely, of all I ever saw, none were more miserable'. On the other side of the hill, the Comte de Merode-Westerloo recalled the weariness that came with defeat as he made his way westwards trying to rally his dispirited men, and, 'Being in the saddle for thirty hours with neither sleep nor food and only one drink of water'. He rode into the square of Höchstädt, to find it crammed with dispirited and disordered French troops, some of whom were slaking their thirst at the town pump, but none paying any attention to mounting a rear-guard action to ward off any pursuit. The Comte set about pulling together a few troopers to bar the road, but a French officer called out as he made off: 'You are very late,' to which Merode-Westerloo replied waspishly that, by comparison, the Frenchman had left the field 'very early'. In the closing moments of a truly terrible day for the French cause, the Comte may be said to have had the last and most pertinent word.

AFTER THE BATTLE

The Spoils of Victory

For all that hot August day the two armies had been in close and deadly combat, and there was no doubting that the day had been a brutally stiff test for all concerned. One army had been beaten and had broken and fled, while the other stood triumphant but exhausted. With the coming of nightfall, Marlborough caught a few hours' sleep in a mill on the edge of Höchstädt that had served the French as a gunpowder store before the battle. Much of the powder was still lying strewn around, but no accident occurred to disturb the Duke's rest. The morning after the battle Marlborough and Prince Eugene made their way to the quarters in Höchstädt that had been hastily allotted to Tallard and his fellow captive generals, and courteously asked after their welfare. The marshal, who was nursing a wounded hand, requested that his own coach be sent for, and Marlborough, sensitive to the very natural sense of dejection in his beaten opponent, agreed to do so. Marshal Marsin and the Elector of Bavaria, meanwhile, continued their withdrawal westwards, and got their own troops and those remnants of Tallard's army that had escaped, across the Danube at Lauingen, and put that watery obstacle between themselves and any immediate pursuit as they made their dejected way towards Ulm. A rearguard was prudently left to burn the bridge if the allies approached.

So much had been achieved, but the cost of the victory was heavy, with Marlborough's wing of the army losing some 9,000 killed and wounded, and that of Eugene 5,000, out of the total of 52,000 deployed on the field of battle; more than one in four of those who had made their way through the defile at Schwenningen had fallen. The losses of the French and Bavarians were even more astonishing, and starkly illustrated the scale of their defeat, amounting to 34,000 (including a staggering tally of nearly 14,000 unwounded prisoners). This figure indicates total tactical defeat. The disaster that had occurred to Tallard's army in the debacle of Blindheim village was further illustrated by the fact that 12,149 of these prisoners were French, while no fewer than forty-two senior and general officers were now captives of the Allies, a sure enough sign of the collapse of their army. John Millner, who fought on the Plain of Höchstädt that day, wrote that the senior prisoners taken were:

PONTOON BRIDGING

All armies in 1704 had an engineer pontoon train to ensure mobility over the many rivers which they would have to cross while on campaign. The few permanent bridges in place would often be either destroyed or held in force by an opponent, so this ability to get across rivers was an important tactical asset. The boats, lined with copper (known as tin-boats) would be carried forward on carts drawn by oxen and moored across a river, stream or marsh, with the plank decking of the bridge laid on top. Once the army had crossed over, the pontoons would be lifted and carted forward to the next water obstacle. The loss of the Bavarian pontoon train after the battle at the Schellenberg was a serious blow to the Elector and his ability to move his army quickly and effectively; the only other option was to use the French pontoons.

Count Tallard, four lieutenant-generals, six major-generals, eight brigadier-generals, three colonels of Horse, three colonels of dragoons, thirteen colonels of Foot, most of them counts, marquises, princes, dukes and barons, besides three Marquises and one captain of the Gens d'Armes.

In a typically generous and compassionate gesture, Marlborough allowed the captive French officers to keep and wear their swords and they were to be treated well, but inevitably the rank and file got rather rougher handling from their victors, and many were stripped of their possessions and occasionally even their clothing.

Among the booty that fell into allied hands were 100 pieces of artillery and mortars, 129 infantry colours and 110 cavalry standards, 5,400 wagons and coaches, 7,000 horses, oxen and mules, the French pontoon train, eight caskets of silver, 3,600 tents and hundreds of sutlers and other camp followers, including some rather exotically dressed 'ladies'. A huge amount of other camp stores, forage, ammunition, food and campaign equipment was taken, and so great was the haul that it could not be counted and gathered in; much had to be left to be pillaged or rot where it lay. The large numbers of prisoners posed an immediate practical problem for the victors, as they had to be guarded, housed (after a fashion) and fed. 'We know not how to dispose of them,' Adam Cardonnel wrote to a friend. 'If we could get well rid of these gentlemen I hope we might soon make an end of the campaign.' Most of those taken captive had fallen to Marlborough's attack, but the duke saw to it that Eugene was allotted a fair share as a part of the spoils of their joint success. Many of these men subsequently volunteered to take service with the imperial army, rather than having to labour in the mines of Austria which was the stark alternative offered.

The war plans of Louis XIV were now in ruins – the Court at Versailles had been enjoying a grandly staged masque, ironically enough intended to celebrate the victory of the River Seine over all the other rivers of Europe, when, Duc de St Simon wrote:

The King received the cruel news of this battle, on the 21 August, by a courier from the Marshal Villeroi. The entire army of Tallard was killed or taken prisoner, it was not known what had become of Tallard himself. Neither the King or anyone could understand, from what reached them, how it was that an entire army had been placed inside a village, and had then surrendered. What was the distress of the King, we were not accustomed to such misfortune.

So great was the shock when the sheer scale of the defeat was confirmed, that some thought that the King had suffered a stroke. A member of the Gens d'Armes, who had been so decisively and repeatedly repulsed that day of battle, wrote in an attempt at explanation of their conduct: 'I charged three times with my brigade [but] I did not see a general officer during the whole battle.' The comment has, of course, to be treated as self-serving and with some caution. John Millner had commented that three French general officers had been killed or mortally wounded on the field, these being the gallant cavalry commander von Zurlauben, the Marquis de Blainville (the son of the great naval reformer, Colbert), and the Marquis de Clerambault, of unfortunate memory.

The French effort to drive Austria out of the war had failed dramatically, and the loss of one of Louis XIV's main field armies could not easily be made good, despite the deep resources of France and that of the King and his people. The military prestige of France that had been so long in the making, was badly damaged, and the Elector of Bavaria, one of the King's main allies, was ruined and became almost a fugitive, while other allies and adherents would not be at all encouraged by this awful turn of events. At another important level, French field commanders, whether or not they had been present in southern Germany that fateful summer, had a grim lesson served to them – the Duke of Marlborough with his ambitious schemes, and the men he led, were dangerous opponents.

The Pursuit

Meanwhile, on the Danube, the allied army, understandably flushed with victory but battered and weary after such efforts, had rested while the wounded were sent to Donauwörth and then on to hospitals in Nördlingen. They only began their pursuit of their beaten opponents on 18 August, but so depleted were some allied regiments, that they could attempt little more without replenishment, and the march was less vigorous than might have been hoped for. The Comte de Merode-Westerloo remembering that: 'If the foe had been quick enough, not one of us would have escaped'. Still, the city of Augsburg was given up shortly after the battle, as were the garrison towns of Memmingen and Biberach, with more stocks of supplies falling into allied hands, and the Margrave of Baden took possession of Ingolstadt – he had missed the day of glory at Blenheim, and regretted the fact, but the fortress was still worth having. The Margrave was summoned to join in the pursuit, but he had forty miles to make up yet, and would not be on the scene with fresh troops for some time.

For their opponents, there could be no early hope of recovery from such a defeat. The French and Bavarians had left Ulm by 21 August other than a small garrison left as a delaying tactic, and abandoning in the process much of their remaining baggage to enable them to make better speed as they withdrew towards the passes of the Black Forest and the Rhine. The allies pushed forward as best they could given the state of the army, while congratulations for the Duke and Eugene on their achievement poured in from many quarters.

The morale of the shocked French and their Bavarian allies was, understandably, badly dented and desertions from the Elector's regiments were numerous, further weakening his ability to continue to campaign as an ally of France with anything like proper effect. The French commander in Alsace, Marshal Villeroi, had come forward to Villingen on 23 August to assist in the withdrawal, an operation he handled very well. Marsin and the

Elector managed to get most of their remaining forces, reduced now to a mere 12,000 strong after casualties and desertions, back across the shelter of the Rhine at Strasbourg by the end of August. Having pushed their march in four columns on parallel roads, Marlborough and Eugene came together at Philippsburg on 5 September, and passed an advanced detachment of troops over the Rhine the next day to occupy a strong position at Speyerbach without any opposition. The Margrave of Baden arrived with his cavalry three days later, and the allied concentration of forces was complete once more. Their next move was anxiously awaited by the French, but a fresh approach to the Elector of Bavaria proposing that he abandon his alliance with France went unheeded, even though it would have restored him to his position.

The surrender of Tallard on the banks of the Danube.

A plan formed by Marlborough to thrust forward to the Moselle valley was thought to be too risky until the army had been fully replenished, and so a siege was to be laid to the French-held fortress of Landau. Baden, typically, was reluctant to take risks, and in this he was probably right, as the forces of Marlborough and Eugene were still well under-strength – much had been achieved but nothing was to be rashly thrown away. Villeroi was also prudently cautious, and could get only modest assistance from Marshal Marsin, so he gave ground at a measured pace, holding the line of the River Quieche until 9 September, and then falling back to a new position at Langencandel, 'Famous for being a strong post,' Marlborough wrote, 'it being covered with thick woods and marshy grounds.'

As the allies advanced, Villeroi withdrew across the river Lauter and then to a position at Hagenau, and the siege of Landau could begin. Ulm had capitulated to Baron Thungen on 11 September and his 14,000 troops were marching to augment the allied army in Alsace. However, the Imperial troops under Baden made slow work of the siege of Landau, where the French garrison, under command of the Marquis de Laubanie, put up a valiant resistance, and the autumn weather turned foul. The fortress did not capitulate until 23 November. Marlborough, meanwhile, had set off with a 12,000 strong detachment of troops in the pay of Queen Anne, across the broken country of the Hornberg to seize Trier on the Moselle river at the end of October, and went on to lay siege to the fortress of Trarbach. Veldt-Marshal Overkirk had marched south with a corps of Dutch troops to meet the Duke, after the triumph at Blenheim no summons would go unanswered while the French were in such disarray. Marlborough left the siege operations to Overkirk and the Prince of Hesse-Cassell, and returned to oversee the siege at Landau, where matters had gone on at a frustratingly measured pace but the fortress at last capitulated on 23 November. The allies had firmly established themselves in Alsace, and the French defensive line on the Rhine was breached, while a base had also been gained in the Moselle valley ready for the resumption of campaigning in 1705. As such, the initiative in the War for the Spanish throne had firmly passed from the French to the Grand Alliance.

The Hero of the Hour

Not surprisingly, Marlborough was the hero of the hour, and after concluding his campaign for the year and sending his troops off to the winter quarters, he visited Berlin, Hanover and The Hague, being received everywhere with great acclaim. Consultation with allies was clearly of the highest importance, but the pace of the Duke's round of visits, after a long and tiring summer, was breathtaking, and he wrote on Thursday, 27 November from Berlin where he had been in consultation with the King in Prussia (as the Elector Frederick was now styled), who provided such excellent troops for the allied armies: 'I shall have my coach ready; but shall not be able to get to Hanover till Monday night, and hope to finish what I have to do there by Wednesday night, so that I may set forward to Holland on Thursday'.

After visiting Hanover and The Hague, the duke then returned to London, in company with Marshal Tallard and thirty-five senior French officers taken captive in August. The reception he received was on the scale of a triumph, and the many colours and standards of the defeated French army were taken in pomp through tumultuous crowds to be displayed in Westminster Hall (where, eventually, they were allowed to rot away to nothing). Parliament, which would have been so savage had he failed, now fawned on the Duke, and the House of Lords gave a solemn address to the returning hero of the hour on the magnitude of his achievement:

Your Grace has not overthrown young and unskilful generals, raw and undisciplined troops, but your Grace has conquered the French and Bavarian armies, that were fully instructed in the arts of war; select veteran troops, flushed with former successes and victories, commanded by generals of great experience and bravery.

A soldier of the Régiment de la Reine, c. 1704. The light grey coat with regimental colour facing was typical of the French troops. Hair was worn long, tied with a ribbon behind the neck.

As a gift from a grateful nation, funds were voted for the building of a great house, sufficient to rival Versailles in its magnificence, on the site of the royal hunting lodge at Woodstock in Oxfordshire, and this in time this became Blenheim Palace, the home of the Duke of Marlborough and his successors to the present day. As a further acknowledgement of his achievement, Marlborough was also made a Prince of the Holy Roman Empire by Emperor Leopold, the consent of Queen Anne to the conferring of such an honour on one of her subjects having been obtained. The principality of Mindleheim was stripped from the now fugitive Elector of Bavaria to provide the necessary estate for the Duke.

Louis XIV lost the ability to win the war that August day in 1704; Tallard's utter defeat on the field of battle and the severe blow to French influence and prestige made sure of that. Such a loss for France was unheard of, but the old king was remarkably resilient and the campaign in 1705 proved a disappointment for the Grand Alliance, with Marlborough's campaign on the Moselle coming to nothing and frustration in the Low Countries and French successes elsewhere. Most notably, French-born King Philip V was proving rather popular with his Spanish subjects, and unless the allies could score some substantial successes in Spain, all else mattered very little. The year 1706 saw a remarkable turnaround, however, with misplaced over-confidence on the part of French commanders leading them to disaster with Marlborough's crowning success

Blenheim Palace viewed from the east.

over Marshal Villeroi at the Battle of Ramillies near to Brussels. The Duke subsequently over-ran the whole Spanish Netherlands in the name of the Austrian claimant to the throne, Archduke Charles (Carlos III), and before long he stood with his troops on the very borders of northern France. In addition, French hopes of success in northern Italy were dashed that autumn, when Prince Eugene and the Duke of Savoy lifted the siege of Turin and killed Marshal Marsin in the process, while allied forces made some gains in Spain after a rather hesitant start.

This all looked very well for the Grand Alliance, but success brought its own problems and while Louis XIV would have now made a judicious peace, the allies had grown greedy and added new demands that could not be borne in Versailles. Perhaps the most significant, and pointless, of these demands was that the Archduke Charles should have the throne in Madrid, never an aim of the Grand Alliance when it was formed in 1701. So the war went wearily on, with successes for Marlborough at Oudenarde (1708) and Malplaquet (1709), and numerous French fortresses of Vauban's intricate design falling into allied hands. Fatally, their cause simultaneously foundered in Spain, where Philip V entrenched his position in Madrid all the more strongly with growing successes in open battle. The allied effort in Spain by contrast was ill-funded and poorly organised, and only ever briefly looked capable of lasting success. This strategic failure fundamentally undermined the allied cause, no matter what gains Marlborough and Eugene might achieve in the Low Countries.

Marlborough fell from grace in December 1711, when he was dismissed from all his offices and posts by an ailing Queen Anne and soon faced charges of peculation and corruption in the handing of army funds. These were politically motivated and largely fabricated accusations which were subsequently not pursued, but the Duke felt it prudent to go and live on the Continent for the time being.

By the summer of 1712, all parties had tired of the war, which had all the appearance of being unwinnable by either side, and of the endless burdensome taxation necessary to pay for the armies. Great Britain concluded terms for peace with France, and in so doing obliged her partners in the Grand Alliance to follow suit. At long last, the war for Spain came to an end; peace was made at the Treaties of Utrecht in 1713, and Baden and Rastadt the following year, and while the French prince remained on the Spanish throne, Austria gained possession of the Southern Netherlands and extensive territories in Italy. In this way, and after much trouble and expense, the main aim of the Grand Alliance when it was formed in 1701, the division of the old Spanish Empire, was achieved.

ORDERS OF BATTLE

All infantry regiments had single battalions present unless otherwise indicated.

The allied (Anglo-Dutch/Imperial) Army Order of Battle

The Left Wing

Commander: John Churchill, 1st Duke of Marlborough

Cutts' Column (on the Left Flank of the allied Army)

Commander: Lord John Cutts of Gowran

Rowe's Brigade (British)

Howe's Regiment
Ingoldsby's Regiment
Churchill's Regiment (Marlborough)
Rowe's Regiment
North & Grey's Regiment

Wilkes' Brigade (Hessian)

Prinz Wilhem's Regiment
Erbrprinz von Hessen-Kassel Regiment
Hessian Grenadier Regiment
Hessian Leibregiment (Guards)
Wartensleben Regiment

Ferguson's Brigade (British)

Derby's Regiment
Ferguson's Regiment
Hamilton's Royal Irish Regiment
2nd Battalion the Royal Regiment (Orkney's)
1st English Foot Guards

St Paul/Hulsen's Brigade (Hanoverian)

De Luc Regiment (Lüneburg-Celle)
De Breuil Regiment (Lüneburg-Celle)
Gauvin Regiment (Hanover)
Hanoverian Guard Regiment (two battalions)

Cavalry support for Cutts

Commander: Lieutenant-General Henry Lumley

Palmes' Cavalry Brigade (British)

Wyndham's (the Queen Dowager's) Regiment of Horse
Wood's Regiment of Horse (one squadron)
Schomberg's Regiment of Horse

Wood's Cavalry Brigade (British)

Lumley's (the Queen's) Regiment of Horse
Wood's Regiment of Horse (one squadron)
Cadogan's Regiment of Horse

Ross's Brigade of Dragoons (British/Hessian)

Ross's Dragoons (Irish Dragoons)
Hay's Scots Dragoons (Grey Dragoons)
Erbprinz von Hessen-Kassel Dragoons

Churchill's Column (centre)

Commander: General Charles Churchill

1st Line Infantry, Left – Ingoldsby

D'Harleville's Brigade (Hessian/Hanoverian)

Schopping Regiment (Hessian)
Stückrad Regiment (Hessian)
D'Herbeville Regiment (Hanoverian)
Von Tozin Regiment (Luneburg/Celle)
Hülsen's Regiment (Hanoverian)

Seckendorff's Brigade (Württemberg)

Stenfels Regiment
Hermann Regiment
Württemberg Grenadier Regiment
Seckendorff's Regiment

1st Line Infantry, Right — Horn

Holstein-Becks' Brigade (Dutch)

Heidebrecht Regiment (Ansbach)
Sturler Regiment (Swiss)
Hirzel Regiment (Swiss)
Recteren Regiment (Dutch)
Goor Regiment (Dutch)

Pallandt's Brigade (Dutch)

Bynheim Regiment (Dutch)
Schwerin Regiment (Prussian)
De Varenne Regiment (Prussian)
Wulffen Regiment (Prussian)

2nd Line infantry — Orkney

Webb's Brigade (British)

Churchill's Regiment
Meredith's Regiment
Webb's (the Queen's) Regiment
1st Battalion the Royal Regiment (Orkney's)

Rantzau's Brigade (Hanoverian)

1st Battalion Rantzau's Regiment (Celle)
2nd Battalion Rantzau's Regiment (Celle)
Bernsdorff's Regiment (Celle)
Teckelenburg Regiment (Hanover)
St Paul Regiment (Hanover)

1st Line Cavalry – Württemberg/von Bulow

Noyelles' Brigade (Hanoverian)

Leib-Horse Cuirassier Regiment
Volgt's Cuirassier Regiment
Noyelles' Cuirassier Regiment

Viller's Brigade (Hanoverian)

Von Bülow's Regiment of Dragoons (Hanover)
Viller's Regiment of Dragoons (Celle)
Bothmar's Regiment of Dragoons (Celle)

Rantzau's Brigade (Danish)

2nd Sjællandske Regiment of Horse
4th Jydske Regiment of Horse
5th Jydske Regiment of Horse
Livregiment Rytter
Württemberg-Ols Dragoons (part)

Brockdorff's Brigade (Danish)

2nd Jysdke Regiment of Horse
3rd Jysdke Regiment of Horse
Ahlefeldt's Cuirassier Regiment
Holstein's Cuirassier Regiment
Württemberg-Ols Dragoons (part)

2nd Line Cavalry – Von Hompesch/Ost-Friese

Hesse-Homburg's Brigade (Hessian)

Leib-Horse Regiment
Spiegel's Carabiniers

Schulemberg's Brigade (Hanoverian)

Schulemburg's Regiment of Dragoons
Breidenbachs' Regiment of Horse

Erbach's Brigade (Dutch)

Erbach's Cuirassier Regiment
Baldwin's Regiment of Horse
Schmettau's Regiment of Dragoons (Ansbach)

Vettinghoff's Brigade (Saxon)

Grevendoff's Regiment of Dragoons
Hardenberg's Regiment of Dragoons
Sachsen-Heilberg Regiment of Horse
Bannier's Regiment of Horse

Auroch's Brigade (Hessian)

Erbach's Regiment of Horse
Auroch's Regiment of Dragoons

The Right Wing

Commander: Prince Eugene of Savoy

1st Line Infantry – Anhalt-Dessau

Finck's Brigade (Prussian)

1st Battalion Grenadier Garde (Kurprinz Freidrich Wilhelm I)
2nd Battalion Grenadier Garde
1st Battalion Margraf Ludwig's Regiment
2nd Battalion Margraf Ludwig's Regiment

1st Battalion Anhalt-Dessau's Regiment
2nd Battalion Anhalt-Dessau's Regiment

Canitz's Brigade (Prussian)

1st Battalion Margraf Philip's Regiment
2nd Battalion Margraf Philip's Regiment
Lieb-Garde Regiment (Lottum's)
1st Battalion Canitz's Regiment
2nd Battalion Canitz's Regiment

Scholten's Column (2nd Line, Right Flank of the allied Army)

Bielke's Brigade (Danish)

1st Battalion Prince George's Regiment
2nd Battalion Prince George's Regiment
2nd Battalion Prince Carl's Regiment
Kongelige Livgarde Regiment

Rebsdorff's Brigade (Danish)

1st Battalion Fynske Regiment
2nd Battalion Sjællandske Regiment
Christian Ulrich's Regiment (Württemberg-Ols)

1st Line Cavalry – Maximilian of Hanover

Natzmer's Brigade (Prussian)

Liebregiment of Dragoons
Margraf Philip's Cuirassier Regiment
Wartensleben Regiment of Horse
Bayreuth-Kulmbach Cuirassier Regiment
Von Krassow's Regiment of Dragoons

Fugger's Brigade (Imperial)

Fugger's Cuirassier Regiment (Swabia)
Alt-Hanover Cuirassier Regiment
Lobkowitz's Cuirassier Regiment

Durlach's Brigade (Imperial)

Limburg-Styrum's Regiment of Dragoons
Württemberg Leib Dragoons
Oettingen's Regiment of Dragoons

2nd Line Cavalry – Württemberg–Teck/De La Tour

L'Ostange's Brigade (Imperial)

L'Ostange's Regiment of Horse
Sonsfeld's Regiment of Dragoons

Bibra's Brigade (Swabian/Palatine)

Helmstaett Cuirassier Regiment
Nagel's Carabinieri Regiment
Venningen's Carabinieri Regiment
Hachenberg's Cuirassiers (one squadron)

Cusani's Brigade (Imperial Austrian)

Fechenbach's Regiment of Dragoons
Württemberg Lieb-Garde Regiment
Bibra's Regiment of Dragoons

Efferen's Brigade (Imperial)

Moorheim's Cuirassier Regiment

Leutsch's Cuirassier Regiment
Von der Ostheim's Cuirassier Regiment

Bayreuth's Brigade (Franconian)

Auffess's Regiment of Dragoons
Bayreuth's Cuirassier Regiment

The French and Bavarian Army

Left Wing — Left Flank

Commander: The Elector of Bavaria

Bavarian Cavalry — Wolframsdorff

Von Weickel's Brigade

Von Weickel's Cuirassier Regiment
D'Arco's Cuirassier Regiment
Garde Karabiniers (one squadron)
Grenadiers a Cheval (one squadron)
Locatelli Hussar Regiment (one squadron)

Von Wolframsdorff's Brigade

Von Wolframsdorff's Cuirassier Regiment
Törring-Seefeld's Regiment of Dragoons
De Costa's Cuirassier Regiment
Bavarian Infantry (Lutzingen village) — Maffei

Maffei's Brigade

Maffei Regiment
Kurprinz Regiment

1st Battalion Leibgarde Fusilier Regiment
2nd Battalion Leibgarde Fusilier Regiment
d'Ocfort Regiment

Mercy's Brigade

Mercy Regiment
Tattenbach Regiment
Von Karthausen Regiment
Von Spilburg Regiment

French Infantry – Left Flank, du Rozel

Fontbeausard's Dragoon Brigade

Régiment de Fontbeausard
Régiment de Listenois
Régiment de la Vrillière

Montbron's Brigade

1st Battalion Régiment de le Dauphin
2nd Battalion Régiment de le Dauphin
3rd Battalion Régiment de le Dauphin
Régiment de Condé
Régiment de Montboissier

Tourouvre's Brigade

Régiment de Lorraine
1st Battalion Régiment de Toulouse
2nd Battalion Régiment de Toulouse

Montmorency's Brigade

Régiment de Béarn
Régiment de Bourbon
Régiment de Nivernais
Régiment de Vermandois

Oberglau Commander: Marshal Marsin

1st Line Infantry (Oberglau village) – de Blainville

Bligny's Brigade

1st Battalion Régiment de Champagne
2nd Battalion Régiment de Champagne
3rd Battalion Régiment de Champagne
Regiment de Saintonge
Nangis's Brigade

1st Battalion Régiment de Bourbonnais
2nd Battalion Régiment de Bourbonnais
Régiment de Foix

2nd Line infantry – de Rozel/Buzancois

Buzancois' Brigade

1st Battalion Régiment de la Reine
2nd Battalion Régiment de la Reine
3rd Battalion Régiment de la Reine
Clare's Brigade (émigré Irish)

Régiment de Clare
Régiment de Dorrington
Régiment de Lee

Choiseul's Brigade

1st Battalion Régiment de Coëtquen
2nd Battalion Régiment de Coëtquen
Régiment de Chartres

Isenghien's Brigade

Régiment de Isenghien (Walloons)
Régiment de Poitou
Régiment de Guyenne
1st Battalion Régiment de Beauferme
2nd Battalion Régiment de Beauferme

1st Line Cavalry – d'Arco

Montmain's Brigade

Régiment de Conde
Régiment de Montmain
Régiment de Bourk (émigré Irish)

Vivan's Brigade

Régiment d'aubusson
Régiment de Vivan
Régiment de Fourquevaux

Conflans' Dragoon Brigade

Régiment de Conflans
Régiment de Rouvray

2nd Line Cavalry – de Legall

Barentin's Brigade

Régiment de Barentin
Régiment de la Billarderie
Régiment de Bissy

Vigier's Brigade

Régiment de Piedmont Royaum
Régiment de Vigier
Régiment de Merinville

Right Wing

Commander: Marshal Tallard

1st Line Infantry (Blindheim village) – Clérambault

de Maulevrier's Brigade

1st Battalion Régiment de Navarre
2nd Battalion Régiment de Navarre
3rd Battalion Régiment de Navarre

Balincourt's Brigade

1st Battalion Régiment de Artois
2nd Battalion Régiment de Artois
Régiment de Provence
Greder's Brigade

1st Battalion Régiment Greder Allemande (German)
2nd Battalion Régiment Greder Allemande
Régiment de Lassay

St Segond's Brigade 1st Battalion Zurlauben Régiment (Walloon)

2nd Battalion Zurlauben Régiment
St Segond Régiment (Italian)

De Angelos' Brigade

1st Battalion Languedoc Régiment
2nd Battalion Languedoc Régiment
1st Battalion Santerre Régiment
2nd Battalion Santerre Régiment

De Hautefeuille's Dragoon Brigade (dismounted)

Régiment de la Méstre de Camp General
Régiment de la Reine
Régiment de Rohan
Régiment de Vasse

1st Line Infantry (drawn into Blindheim)

Régiment de Fusiliers d'Artillerie (some accounts only)

Montroux's Brigade

Montroux Régiment (Italian)
1st battalion Aunis Guienne Régiment
2nd Battalion Aunis Guienne Régiment
Montfort's Brigade

1st Battalion Montfort Régiment (Walloon)
2nd Battalion Montfort Régiment
Régiment de Agentois (some accounts only)
Blaisois Régiment

Denonville's Brigade

1st Battalion Régiment du Roi
2nd Battalion Régiment du Roi
3rd Battalion Régiment du Roi
1st Battalion Boulonnais Régiment
2nd Battalion Boulonnais Régiment

2nd Line Infantry – Montpreyoux

Trecesson's Brigade

1st Battalion Régiment de Robecque (Walloon)
2nd Battalion Régiment de Robecque Régiment d'Albaret

Breuil's Brigade

1st Battalion Régiment d'Auxerrois
2nd Battalion Régiment d'Auxerrois Régiment de Chabrillant

Bellisle's Brigade

Régiment de Nice
Régiment de Tavannes
Régiment de Bandeville

1st Line Cavalry – von Zurlauben

Vertilly's Brigade

Gendarmerie de France

Broglie's Brigade

Régiment du Roi
Régiment de Tarneau
Régiment de la Beaune

Grignan's Brigade

Régiment Méstre de Camp General
Régiment de Grignan

2nd Line Cavalry – d'Humieres

Merode-Westerloo's Brigade (Walloon)

Régiment de Caetano
Régiment de Acosta
Régiment de Heider

La Valliere's Brigade

Régiment de Bourgogne
Régiment de la Valliere
Régiment de Noailles
Régiment de Beringhen

Silly's Brigade

Régiment d'Orléans
Régiment de Montreval
Régiment de St Poutanges
Régiment de Ligonday

FRENCH OFFICERS 'OF NOTE' TAKEN PRISONER AT BLENHEIM

(Taken from Lediard Volume I, 1735)

Duc de Tallard (General officer commanding, Marshal of France)
Marquis de Marivaux (Lieutenant-General)
Marquis de Hautefille (General of Dragoons)
Marquis de Blanzac (Lieutenant-General, Marechal de Camp)
Marquis d'Enonville (Lieutenant-General)
Marquis de Valiere (Brigadier-General of Cavalry)
Marquis de Silly (Brigadier-General of Cavalry)
Marquis de Joury (Brigadier-General of Dragoons)
Marquis de Massiliers (Brigadier-General of Gens d'Armes)
Le Chevalier de Croissi (Brigadier-General of Infantry)
Marquis de St Second (Brigadier-General of Infantry)
Marquis de Signey (Brigadier-General of Infantry)
Marquis de Montfort (Brigadier-General of Infantry)

Blenheim 1704

Marquis de Septville (Brigadier-General of Gens d'Armes)
Marquis de Sassenage (Aide de Camp – Tallard's son in law)
Marquis de Nonan (Colonel of Dragoons)
Marquis de Pouange (Colonel of Cavalry)
Le Chevalier d'Ligonday (Colonel of Cavalry)
Marquis de Vassy (Colonel of Cavalry)
Comte de Tovannes (Colonel of Infantry)
Comte de Lionne (Colonel of Infantry)
Marquis de Lassy (Colonel of Infantry)
Baron d'Elston (Colonel of Infantry)
Marquis de Montperoux (Marechal de Camp)

BIBLIOGRAPHY AND FURTHER READING

(*JSAHR – Journal of the Society for Army Historical Research*)

Alison, A., *Military Life of the Duke of Marlborough*. (Harper & Brothers, NY, 1848)

Atkinson, C., *Marlborough and the Rise of the British Army*. (Putman, London, 1921)

Belloc, H., *The Tactics and Strategy of the Great Duke of Marlborough* **(NRC, 1933)**

Chandler, D. (ed.), *Military Memoirs, Robert Parker and Comte de Merode-Westerloo*. (Longman Green ,London, 1968)

Marlborough as Military Commander (1974)

The Art of Warfare in the Age of Marlborough **(Butsford, 1976)**

A Journal of the Spanish Succession War (JSAHR) (1984)

Churchill, W., *Marlborough, His Life and Times* **(Harrap & Co. Ltd, Lonond,** 1933)

Crichton, A. (ed.), *The Life and Diary of Lieutenant-Colonel J Blackader* **(Edinburgh,** 1824)

Dalton, C., *The Blenheim Roll* (1904)

Falkner, J., *Great and Glorious Days* (THP, Stroud, 2002)

Blenheim, Marlborough's Greatest Victory, 1704 (Leo Cooper,2004)

Marlborough's Wars, Eye-Witness Accounts (Leo Cooper, 2005)

Fortescue, J., *History of the British Army*, Vol I (MacMillan, London, 1899)

The Life and Adventures of Mrs Christian Davies (Mother Ross), (Peter Davies, London, 1929)

Frischauer, P., *Le Prince Eugene* (1933)

Green, D., *Blenheim* (Country Life, Oxford, 1975)

Henderson, N., *Prince Eugen of Savoy* (Weidenfield & Nicholson, 1964)

Horsley, W. (tr. and ed.), *Chronicles of an Old Campaigner* (John Murray, London, 1904)

Kane, R., *The Campaigns of King William and Queen Anne* (J. Millan, London, 1745)

Kemp, A., *The Weapons and Equipment of the Marlborough Wars* (Blanford Press, 1980)

Lang, G., *Orders of Battle for the Schellenberg, 1704, and Blenheim 1704*, (unpublished mss), seen by the author 1997 and 2000

Langallerie, M., *Memoires of the Marquis de Langallerie* (N. Cliff, London, 1710)

Lediard, T., *Life of the Duke of Marlborough* (1736)

MacMunn, J., *Prince Eugene, Twin Marshal with Marlborough* (S. Low, London, 1934)

McBane, D., *The Expert Swordsman's Companion* (Glasgow, 1729)

Millner, J., *A Compendious Journal* (1752)

Murray, G. (ed.), *The Letters and Despatches of the Duke of Marlborough* (John Murray, London, 1845)

Nosworthy, B., *The Anatomy of Victory* (Hippocrene Books, USA, 1992)

Phelan, I., *Marlborough as Logistician*, (JSAHR, 1989–90)

Pigaillem, H., *Blenheim 1704 Le Prince Eugene et Marlborough contre la France* (Economica, 2004)

Sichart, R. von, *Geschichte der Koniglich-Hannoverschen Armee* (Hannover, 1866)

Taylor, F., *The Wars of Marlborough* (Basil Blackwell, London, 1921)

Trevelyan, G., *Select Documents for Queen Anne's Reign* (Cambrige University Press, Cambridge, 1929)
England Under Queen Anne, Blenheim (Metheusen & Co. Ltd, London, 1933)

Verney, P., *Blenheim* (Batsford, 1976)

Notes on the Orders of Battle at Blenheim (Liddle Hart Centre, King's College, London). 2013

INDEX